Becoming a

Radiologic Technologist

A Student's Guide: from Choosing the Right School to Jump Starting Your Career

By Jeremy Enfinger, ARRT(R)

Becoming a Radiologic Technologist A Student's Guide: from Choosing the Right School to Jump Starting Your Career

Printed in the United States of America

ISBN-13: 978-1478170440
ISBN-10: 1478170441

Learn more information at:
http://bloggingradiography.blogspot.com

For my family, who has supported every endeavor I have undertaken.

Presented to:

_____

From:

_____

Contents

Introduction:

So you are interested in applying to x-ray school and your ambition is heightened. Congratulations! You are about to embark on an adventure that will challenge you and educate you. It will equip you with valuable skills that provide a firm career foundation and plenty of room to grow. Many schools can prepare you to learn the skills of a technologist and provide all of the information that you need to pass the national radiography registry exam, but there are other components that you will need to master along the way to be successful. In this book, you will learn about the misconceptions most people have about what x-ray techs do. There is a lot of false information available that may misguide you to choose the wrong x-ray program. I reveal the appropriate research methods for selecting an accredited radiography program without spending unneeded time or money on an education that will fail to qualify you for the job you want. Learn the characteristics that instructors, technologists, and potential employers are seeking and gain a competitive edge. You are about to begin a two-year job interview. Every decision and action you make throughout your clinical experience will be observed and considered when you graduate from x-ray school and begin your search for a job. There are plenty of students accepted into radiography programs with the skills to obtain ARRT registration, but I will explain how to stand out among them.

Part I: Before School

Chapter 1: Myths about What Radiologic Technologists Do

One of my largest motivators for writing this book is to clear up any misconceptions about what a radiologic technologist does every day. In my experience, there is a common misunderstanding among new students, the general public, patients, nurses, etc. that an x-ray tech's day consists of placing an injured body part on the x-ray table, then disappearing behind a wall to push a button. This process is believed to be repeated hundreds of times per day over the duration of an eight-hour shift, and we go home to collect a whopping paycheck at the end of the week.

I'm making a bit of an effort to be dramatic, but it's not too far from the truth when discussing aspects of the career with people who have not researched the field. I run into people in the medical field every day who do not truly grasp the educational background and thought process required to perform an x-ray examination.

My intent is to educate and inform anyone who is interested in pursuing radiologic technology as a career. I only ask that candidates do some homework and have a realistic informed approach prior to jumping through the hoops to begin an educational program in radiography. Reading this book is a great start!

It would save potential candidates a lot of trouble if there were a way to evaluate what actually occurs in the typical day for a radiologic technologist. If you're reading this book, that means there is a good chance that you are already considering x-ray school. And if you are considering x-ray school, then you probably already have some ideas about what an x-ray tech does that you have considered appealing. As appealing as it may seem to be, you cannot know what it is like to be an x-ray tech until you actually become one, but I think it's safe to say that you have developed some expectations.

I don't wish to discourage anyone from pursuing their dream of becoming a radiographer, but I have seen some unrealistic perceptions about what we do in the radiology department. Here are some myths that I have heard over the years from students during their first weeks in the clinical setting:

Myth #1: "X-ray techs don't work with blood or guts"

In fact, x-ray techs see a lot of blood. We perform procedures in trauma centers in which you may be asked to image and care for patients with open wounds, lacerations, impaled body parts, compound fractures (bones broken and sticking out through the skin), hemoptysis (vomiting blood), stab wounds, gunshot wounds, car accident victims, etc. To put it simply, all of the situations you may encounter when watching a medical television drama typically require an x-ray examination of some kind.

In most states, you need to learn how to use a needle to access a vein, a necessary skill to perform injections. In advanced modalities like interventional radiology, you may be scrubbing in with a physician and assisting with some fairly invasive procedures. Diagnostic x-ray techs are needed daily in the operating room, where you will get a first-hand view of the internal organs of the human body and see a great deal of blood.

Myth #2: *"X-ray techs don't have to clean up messes"*

We are responsible for care of the patient when they are undergoing a radiographic examination. We may not be responsible for the patient for twelve hours per day like a nurse, but from the time the patient enters our department until they leave, we are responsible for their care. This includes assisting patients that need to use a bedpan, which may be nauseated and vomiting and may need gowns or linens changed.

We perform some messy procedures like BE's, which is short for "barium enema." This is a common procedure for a radiologic technologist to conduct that involves insertion of a flexible tube into a patient's rectum, and allowing a bag of contrast (barium) attached to the tube to drain into the intestine to fill it. This process allows the radiologist to see the large intestine on x-ray since we normally cannot view very much detail in the intestine on a plain x-ray without contrast.

Another procedure that can be messy is naso-gastric tube insertion. For some patients who cannot hold food down, or who may need food liquefied for digestion, we insert a long tube into a nostril and feed it down to the stomach while watching it on x-ray to make sure the tube ends up in the correct location. Sometimes we go past the stomach into the small intestine, but x-ray is required to confirm that the tip of the tube is in the right position. Occasionally the tube can coil back toward the nose, or even enter the lungs. The last thing you want to do is pump fluid through a tube into the lungs causing a patient to drown, so confirmation of tube placement under x-ray guidance is a valuable service.

You will be asked to clean up a variety of messes which may contain an array of various bodily fluids during an average day in the average hospital. You may be able to avoid such a scenario for a while, but sooner later, it's a matter of statistical probability that your patient will need assistance in one of these areas on your watch. Trust me when I tell you that the odds are not in your favor for messes like these to be avoidable.

Myth #3: *"X-ray techs don't need to know math"*

In fact, a majority of what we do relies on basic algebraic functions. We need to be able to calculate radiation exposure factors using expensive and fairly complex equipment. There are variables to account for like patient size, what type of equipment is being used, the location the exams are being performed, and different pathologies that we need to be educated about that all require adjustments in our calculations. We also use math to determine dosage when administering contrast media. Math is at the heart of what we do every day, and it is necessary to have a thorough understanding of it to prevent overexposure of radiation to our patients, to promote high standards of patient safety, and to ensure that we produce images of the highest medical quality with the minimum number of attempts.

Myth #4: *"Being an x-ray tech is easy"*

Anything that someone does very well will appear "easy". X-ray techs can often be *perceived* as being behind the scenes or somehow hidden behind the camera, interacting with patients or hospital staff on a limited basis. This unfortunately causes a common misconception that our work is easy, or effortless. Although a good radiographer may make it appear to be easy, there is a lot of theory and skill behind every action. There are also many things that patients and other health care workers do not see us do.

I'll be the first to admit that physically speaking, digging ditches or lifting bales of hay for eight hours a day would be much more challenging, and I would prefer a technologist's job over manual labor like that any day. We do have a bit of physical labor that we must be able to accomplish though. Pushing around heavy portable equipment and placing image receptors underneath patients that weigh several hundred pounds can do tend to strain your lower back after a busy day. We need to know and practice proper body mechanics to prevent injury. All it takes is one small twist or turn to do some major damage on your body, especially if it is a repetitive motion that you need to perform hundreds of times per day.

There is also a lot of educational background that we need to possess to perform our work well. Being able to understand and apply complex ideas in a real-time and sometimes stressful environment every day does not come easily to everyone. Radiography school is designed to prepare you with the basic knowledge to make you employable as a radiologic technologist. Any honest tech will admit that it takes a few years of full-time employment after school is over to feel comfortable with what you are doing, and even still, situations occur that are unexpected. There is a lot of scientific knowledge that we must possess, as well as the flexibility to think outside of the box to acquire images on patients that cannot be positioned exactly like the textbooks show, and this can sometimes take years to master.

Think about a point-and-shoot camera that a random person takes pictures with, and then compare those pictures to the ones in Time Magazine made by a professional photographer. The difference is obvious. We are professionals, and instead of using a camera to take photographs of patients which would be completely harmless, we use radiation to acquire our images. Any radiation dose poses a potential risk to the person receiving it, and proper education is imperative for those administering it to meet professional and safety standards. In other words, there is the possibility to inflict physical harm with what we do, so we better know what we're doing before being released into the field on our own.

Myth #5: "X-ray techs do not have to administer CPR"

It is not quite as common for a radiologic technologist to administer CPR on a patient compared to a nurse, but it does happen occasionally in one's career. Including all of my patient care experience (I was a transporter before getting my x-ray license) of almost 20 years, I have performed CPR maybe a dozen times. I have initiated or participated in a "code blue" (when there's no heart beat or breathing) at least 50 times. Reemphasizing "myth #2", the patient is in our care until we hand care off to another professional. We don't get to walk away and let someone else initiate a code or start CPR if you are the only person with the patient at the time. You will be expected to follow the protocol that you will be taught in school, and at your hospital for situations like this. Thankfully, as a student, you will always be supervised and will not be left hanging out to dry in the event of a "code blue."

If I haven't managed to scare you away from the field of radiologic technology yet, I think you will enjoy the field as long as you are open to a few things; an ever-changing environment in which you can learn new technology, a chance to make a difference in the treatment that patients receive in a hospital or outpatient environment, and an opportunity to express creativity while maintaining quality in your work. I have been fortunate to find myself in a rewarding career all in itself, with the added benefit of being a stepping stone to advanced opportunities and multiple career destinations.

Chapter 2: The Demand for Radiologic Technologists

There has been some conflicting information released over the last few years about the job outlook for radiologic technologists. The ASRT (American Society of Radiologic Technologists) published a survey in 2011 which concluded the number of open positions actively being recruited for, or vacancy rate, has dropped from 10.3% in 2003 to 2% in 2011. This seems to conflict with what the Bureau of Labor Statistics estimates. They predict there will be career growth of 28% between the years 2010 and 2020 (http://www.bls.gov/ooh/healthcare/radiologic-technologists.htm#tab-1).

So what are we supposed to believe when conflicting information arises from two very trusted resources? Well, it's going to be up to you to do some research on the job market in your region. I hear mixed reports from across the country about how easy or difficult it is to find a job, and it is always wise to research employment rates in the areas you would consider working. No matter what predictions we come across based on varying data, they are still just predictions, and predictions stand a great chance to be inaccurate.

Much of what we are experiencing with the career outlook we today is because of a prediction. It has been well-known for a few years now that the baby boomer generation currently composes the largest percentage of people in the work force. As of 2011, this population has already begun reaching the age of 65, and some have started retiring already. This was the easy part of a prediction that influenced our field today.

Here's the part that was difficult to predict: Due to the economy, a great percentage of the baby boomer population that everyone anticipated would begin retirement over the last few years have avoided it. Their savings and investments do not currently hold the value that they once did. It makes perfect sense for them to avoid dipping into savings and retirement accounts as long as possible. By continuing to work, it instills much more financial security for potential retirees to continue to bring home a paycheck when it is difficult to see an end in sight to the struggling economy.

I personally remember a technologist who liked to flaunt that he was "ready for retirement" on a regular basis. When I graduated x-ray school in May of 2000, I worked with him occasionally during his regular shift from 11:00 p.m. until 7:30 a.m., and he really liked to talk about all of his investments in stocks and bonds. I didn't know what to think at the time because I was brought up to treat these topics with the utmost discretion. His plans were to work through December of 2001 and retire happily in January of 2002. Then, something happened that no one predicted on September 11, 2001. The world was caught off-guard at the coordinated multiple hijackings of passenger planes, two of which were flown into the World Trade Center buildings. If you weren't around to witness the news coverage, I'm certain you have seen many haunting images and videos from media coverage of that horrible day.

What we typically don't think about when this subject is brought up was the after-effect on the stock market. It crashed... and it crashed big time. The technologist that liked to flaunt his "several hundred thousand dollars in savings and investments" was also very vocal about his less than forty thousand dollars that his earnings had dwindled down to almost overnight. Whether any of his coworkers believed that his previous bragging about his earnings was inappropriate, no one could avoid feeling horribly about his situation. He ended up working an additional seven or eight years and still retired with much less than before the September 11 attacks. Though we've managed to bounce back as a nation, there are still ways that our country is still seeing the financial aftermath from that tragedy.

The problem we will soon be facing in the job market is two-fold. The largest percentage of employees in the work force, the boomers, will soon leave their leadership roles vacant. We need to be training currently employed health care professionals now to fill those positions once they become vacant. We also need to be training and hiring new grads to fill the positions of those moving up.

At the same time that we will be losing employees in the work force, we will also be seeing a rise in the elderly patient population. At what point will we decide it's the appropriate time to proactively balance the work-force? If we wait to train technologists until a shortage exists, we cannot possibly expect to meet the needs of our patient population. The difficult part to predict is when we should recruit in order to prevent a health care crisis and a shortage of technologists while we grow our patient population.

While the prospects for jobs are not as plentiful as they used to be in 2003, there are still opportunities. Radiologic technology is not a field that is going to disappear. It is competitive, but not impossible to find work. I wouldn't discourage anyone from pursuing a career that they have a passion for just because there is competition. Weigh the risks vs. benefits for yourself. If you aren't certain this is the career path for you, you might not want to risk two years of your life to try it out. But if you decide to go for it, make sure your performance is one that makes you invaluable to an employer. You want to be the type of employee that will put everything you've got into being a great technologist.   Decide that you are going to master every skill and continue learning new skills to improve your professional worth and marketability.

It may take some time and patience in today's market to obtain full-time employment or your "ideal" job as a technologist, but in the next few years we will see the largest need for health care workers in decades. It will take a few years to see a market where you can walk into any hospital and obtain employment, but there's still opportunity for those who truly commit themselves and strive for excellence.

Chapter 3: Questions to Consider

Before you make a final decision on diagnostic radiography as your career choice, it is imperative to step back and evaluate whether or not you are making the right decision for yourself. The last thing any patient-centered career needs is individuals who are in it for the wrong reasons. If you have any misconceptions about what you are about to submerge yourself into, there's a great chance that you will not be happy, let alone content.

Here is a list of questions to ask think about:

1. Do I value people, and am I ready to commit myself to a career of service?
2. Am I financially prepared to commit at least two years to a full-time responsibility on top of my current responsibilities?
3. Can I care for other people with different beliefs and life styles?
4. Can I provide the same level of care to people who are angry or rude, and sometimes physically combative?
5. Can I treat everyone with respect, regardless of the respect they show me?

6. Have I properly researched an accredited school for radiography (see Chapter 5)?
7. Do I have a support system in place if I need help?
8. Do I know enough about the job market to be comfortable with finding employment after school?
9. Have I researched the salary I can expect to be paid as a technologist once employed?
10. Am I comfortable interacting with patients?
11. Am I capable of working in a fast-paced environment?
12. Can I multi-task?
13. Can I tolerate all of the things I may see in a hospital setting?
14. Who will be affected by all the requirements that school will need (spouse, dependents, family, etc)?
15. Am I willing to work any shift, including nights, overnight, weekends and holidays for a while in order to land my first job?
16. Can I afford to be out of work for a while after school if I don't find a job right away?
17. Am I willing to be on-call?
18. Can I put myself out there to learn new things in uncomfortable situations?
19. Can I conduct myself in a professional manner?
20. Can I afford tuition?
21. Do I have reliable transportation to get to and from my clinical assignment?

22. Do I have the ability to learn about different computer software?
23. Can I work well individually, as well as in a team environment?
24. Am I already comfortable with or comfortable learning algebra-level math?
25. Can I remain calm in emergency situations?

If you answered "yes" to most of these questions, you are most likely headed down the right path to a career that you will flourish in. If you answered "no" or you were not sure, then you may want to pursue further research or consider a different career path – I'm sure you have an idea which option will apply most to you in your situation. I did not write this book to try to promote my field to everyone, and I certainly don't expect to have a New York Times best-seller. I simply want to provide accurate information to people who are sincere in researching radiography as a career option, and I would like to do whatever I can to encourage those who have a true desire to pursue it.

Chapter 4: Types of Radiography Programs

There are generally six types of programs available today. They are community college-based, private college-based, four-year bachelor degree programs, hospital-based (which will soon be phased out), and online programs.

I attended a community college program at Cypress College in Cypress, CA. I have been a full-time classroom instructor, full-time clinical instructor, and an adjunct instructor for two community college-based educational plans (Wake Technical Community College in Raleigh, NC and San Diego Mesa College in San Diego, CA). Acceptance into different community colleges varies, but many have waiting lists. Some waiting lists can be up to three or four years, and some are available right away if you have successfully completed your prerequisite courses. Other entrance methods include a lottery system in which all eligible applicants are randomly selected if there are more applicants than there are seats in the program. In both methods, GPA in prerequisite courses is important. Either way, the community college programs are usually the cheapest when comparing tuition unless you have moved within the last year. If you have not established residency within the state you are currently living in, which takes one year, then tuition can often be similar to a four-year university. If you have established residency, tuition and books combined can cost as little as a few thousand dollars.

Private colleges are typically much easier to gain acceptance to. I began my teaching experience at PIMA Medical Institute in Mesa, AZ. There were some obvious differences compared to what I was used to. There are not often as long waiting lists, but you may need to interview for some programs. There are several methods, including those already mentioned with community college programs that are used to grant students entry into a private college. As usual, GPA is considered, but tuition is usually much higher and can reach tens of thousands of dollars. The advantage; no wait list and usually better student to teacher ratio. You will get more one-on-one instruction and availability of instructors. Due to the Montgomery GI Bill, I have noticed that a lot of military veterans tend to sign up for private college programs because the military pays their way. Not a bad deal if you ask me.

There is a growing number of four year schools that do everything that a two year program does to get you qualified for the ARRT registry exam, but they have additional curriculum above and beyond that is designed to set you up for success later in your career. Although I graduated from a community college program in 2000, I began teaching in 2005 and knew that a bachelor degree requirement was soon coming (and is currently in existence) to be able to continue teaching in the classroom of an accredited school of radiography. I chose to do a degree completion program through Florida Hospital College of Health Sciences (now called Adventist University of Health Sciences) completely online. They also offer a traditional radiography program if you want to go from zero to Bachelor of Science in one location, as well as many other allied health programs.

The going trend of our field is a continuous increase in the level of professionalism and educational standards. Though these bachelor degree programs are relatively new, expect to see more offered in the next 10 years. If you happen to complete x-ray school by any other means, most of the four year schools offer degree completion programs to graduates holding an associate degree and current ARRT registration.

One of the options that are becoming increasingly rare these days is a hospital based program. These focus primarily on more clinical hours, with time taken out from the hospital setting to have classes, and they are often taught at the hospital itself. A large number of these programs disappeared a few years ago when the standards of education increased by requiring an associate degree as part of an accredited school. The traditional hospital based program provided students with a certificate instead of the degree. A few of these programs still remain that have been able to accommodate for the new requirements by affiliating themselves with a local college to supplement an associate degree education. When researching a school, you need to make sure that any hospital based program has something like this in place otherwise you will not be eligible to take the registry examination.

There are also a few online programs that are accredited by the Joint Review Committee on Education in Radiologic Technology (JRCERT). They are typically associated with campus-based programs that are already accredited, but may require special circumstances for enrollment. PIMA Medical Institute for example offers an "Advanced Placement Track Radiography Program"
(http://pmi.edu/online/careers/online_rad.asp)
to individuals who have prior education in radiography and have ability to be observed by an ARRT registered technologist to ensure competency of exams performed. Eligibility to these types of programs is extremely strict, and cannot be offered to students with no prior training or professional practice.

Finally, and the most recent method for completing an accredited program that I have learned of is through the military. The Air Force, Army, and Navy have programs, and you can find more information at https://www.arrt.org/education/military. But it should be very clear that just because you enlist in the military, you are not guaranteed a specialty of your choice. You may be able to learn on-the-job in some branches, but if you find that you have the opportunity to attend their accredited program, you should make every effort to do so.

The big difference between someone who learns on the job and someone who takes the extra time to attend the military's accredited program is the ability to take the ARRT registry exam. If you are already in the military but may be discharged soon because you are near the completion of your service contract, you should seriously consider your options if it is still possible for you to attend their training program.

If you wait until you are discharged from the military, you can certainly use your GI Bill to attend school, but you will also have to get on a wait list and take some prerequisite courses in order to qualify for application. This can take several years if you do not choose a private college. Don't neglect thinking about the long-term either. Where would you end up in 10 years? Here are a couple of options:

Option 1: leave the military and find a civilian school to attend. If you get into a private college right away (best case scenario if you want to finish quickly), you will most likely need to work while you attend a radiography program with its full-time requirements. In two to three years you could be a registered technologist, but a private school would consume a lot of your GI Bill. You begin to gain experience in the field, and if it takes you five years of tech experience to be able to move into a supervisory role, that would happen seven to eight years after your military discharge. It might take longer if you don't have a bachelor's degree.

Option 2: stay in the military and attend their school. You may have to sign up for an extra couple of years, but you will be discharged with eligibility to take the ARRT registry exam right away, if you haven't already passed the exam while still in service. Your GI Bill can be used for a bachelor's degree or additional education like advanced modality training. You could realistically work as a radiologic technologist during your additional education and have four or five years of tech experience under your belt when you obtain your degree. Ideally, after that much experience, you should be able to move into a supervisory role if that's a direction you are considering, and you would have the education to support your qualifications. 10 years from discharge, it is not improbable that you could be in a management role.

This is by no means a limitation of your options. I have only compared two options from a multitude of scenarios that might fit your situation, and I think you could write an entire book based on the possibilities that apply to each individual. My goal was to demonstrate what kind of a thought process one should assume when selecting a program.

These two options have very few variables as well. Anyone reading this book will have to personalize their variables, which will realistically be far more numerous than these simple examples. One person might have a wife and six children to provide for. Another person may have a dependent parent living with them while considering their potential for attending radiography school. Someone right out of high school who can attend school while living with parents will have a very different approach to choosing the right program for them.

The point is you have to look at all of the variables that apply directly to you and those you are responsible for. I would highly encourage anyone reading this book to have a long conversation about how going to school might affect those around you. You will need a lot of support in school, and it could place a strain on relationships, especially if you are going to be working while in school.

I know that if it weren't for my parents, going to school would have been a lot more difficult than it actually was for me. This is not just an investment in *your* future; it is also an investment in the futures of those you are responsible for. They are key stakeholders in this decision and will probably be making sacrifices right along with you in order to contribute to your success.

You will need to research the x-ray programs available to you and determine which ones you would consider attending. Then you can fill in the gaps with valuable information about these schools such as wait list time, tuition cost, pass rate percentages, accreditation standing, time required for program completion, and the amount of prerequisites required. This is the information that you should share with those who will be investing in your future with you.

Chapter 5: Researching Radiography Schools

Whether this is something you have always wanted to do, if it is a new interest, or you are choosing radiography as a second career, knowing how to select a school is vital to your success. If you have already been accepted into a radiography program, you may still want to read these chapters to make sure you have enrolled in the right school that will help you get the job you want.

There are many schools out there that are marketing themselves to be something that they are not. In this chapter, I explain how to become an unrestricted x-ray tech or more specifically, a radiologic technologist. This is a key term when searching for the appropriate program. Simply saying train to be an "x-ray tech" does not guarantee that the appropriate accreditation has been issued to the institution that is advertising in this manner. If you follow my blog, you already know that I considered placing the term "x-ray tech" in the title to this book. Although it can sometimes be used as an abbreviated version of "technologist," it is common among the general public to describe my profession. That's why so many sites are popping up with information without using the term "technologist"… people don't always know to search for it, therefore they can easily be misled if they do not know the difference. Training to be an "x-ray technician" has a completely different meaning than "radiologic technologist" in the United States. Let's define the two before moving onto the next step.

An *X-Ray Technician* can be defined in different ways. One way describes those who work on x-ray equipment. The other more common definition is a person who has been trained to perform a specific skill. In this example, a technician knows how to take an x-ray, usually of limited body parts, and may or may not have a formal registration or license. A *Radiologic Technologist* is someone who has a degree in, and possesses expertise in performing radiographic examinations. A technologist performs diagnostic exams with no limitation of anatomy, understands the physics and potential risks of ionizing radiation, and has been trained to safely operate stationary and mobile x-ray equipment including fluoroscopy (live x-ray), utilizing the least amount of radiation necessary to produce the highest quality of images. In the U.S., a radiologic technologist has passed the ARRT registry examination and students graduate with at least an associate degree in the subject, and sometimes a bachelor's degree.

There are x-ray programs that grant their graduates a limited license to perform some x-ray exams, and I believe those programs are valuable within their scope, but this book describes how to become a *Radiologic Technologist*.

So how do you know if the school you would like to apply to meets the requirements for graduates to become radiologic technologists? This is vital: The school must be accredited by the Joint Review Committee on Education in Radiologic Technology (JRCERT).   Their website can be found at www.jrcert.org where there is a searchable database for accredited radiography programs.   Make sure that the school that you are considering is on this list. If it isn't, then you will not be qualified to take the ARRT registry examination upon graduation, and you will not be qualified to become a technologist.

When I began writing this book, the JRCERT website only included a database of accredited programs. They have now updated their website with some additionally valuable information for researching schools.   You can now find registry exam pass-rate statistics for each school. They also list employment statistics of each school's graduates after completion of their respective x-ray programs.   Make sure to bookmark their website and regularly check for updated information while you are taking your prerequisite courses.

There are some technical schools that are very misleading about how they market their x-ray programs, and unfortunately, I have seen many people pay thousands, or sometimes tens of thousands of dollars only to find that they are not qualified for the job that they had hoped to be able to perform. If advertisements say "Become an x-ray technician", this should be a red flag to you indicating that they do not offer a fully accredited program. There are some states, like California, that have special certifications for limited licensed technologists. The scope of practice for limited licensed technologists varies from state to state, but is typically limited to chest x-rays, possibly spine x-rays and extremities like hands and feet and do *not* include mobile x-ray or fluoroscopic examinations. These schools will teach their students how to position body parts properly and how to make adjustments to some of the image qualities, but vary in educational requirements in physics, quality control, and radiation protection compared to a JRCERT-accredited program. Meticulous detail about the "how" and "why" explanations regarding physics, x-ray equipment and all of its functions, as well as effects of radiation on the human body need to be included to become a *technologist*.

Once you know that your school of choice is on the list of JRCERT-accredited institutions, you should do some research about which school would best fit your learning style and needs. Try to find out what other schools are in your area and compare pass-rate statistics. The program director for each of the schools is listed on the

JRCERT website, as well as their contact information. But with the new website, you no longer need to contact them to learn this information. The school can lose its accreditation with JRCERT if the pass rate drops below 75%. If a school does this, they usually go on probation with JRCERT for one year, and if the following years' scores are below 75%, accreditation gets dropped. You definitely don't want to be in the middle of your program when accreditation gets dropped because you will not be able to take your registry exam upon completion. You can contact JRCERT to ask if the school has any history of being in probation. In my personal opinion, the school you apply to should score at least within the 90 percentile range, and preferably closer to 100%. If you attend an information session for any of your perspective schools, these are two things that you should ask. It's a good idea to check with JRCERT after the information session to confirm that what you are told is the truth.

You can also ask what kind of retention rates their program has. In other words, how many students drop out or fail out of their program once enrolled. This could indicate trouble as well. A good school may have a retention rate of about 75% to 100% on average over the past 5 years, with the exception of a bad year every once in a while. If the school has below a 60% retention rate, this is another red flag that something is wrong.

Again, this is my personal opinion, so you should consult more than one person on this subject. It always helps to do a quick internet search for reviews of each radiography program you are considering. It would definitely be preferred for you to speak face to face with graduates if possible, and I have heard of some programs inviting graduates to speak at information sessions or orientations. You may ask the program directors for graduate contacts, but keep in mind that they will most likely refer you to their "star" students who had excellent experiences throughout their program. I have had potential students tell me that they placed an advertisement on social networking sites asking for feedback which proved rather candid. Choose a site that allows announcements to be made for free in your local state, county and even city. You and the person you question have the advantage of anonymity, which should promote honesty because neither party has anything to lose for stating their opinions.

The other attribute to consider is the employment rate of graduates. A school that cannot provide employment statistics of 75% of students having jobs within 6 months after graduation will be required to reduce the number of accepted students into their program. If you ask for the last 5 years of employment statistics for the different schools you are attending, you can probably notice a trend. If a particular school has maintained accreditation, but has fewer and fewer students accepted into their program every year, it is possible that the school may potentially cut that program in the future. You want a school that has high ARRT exam pass rates, a 75%-100% retention rate, and one that has maintained the number of students accepted into the program, if not an increase in that number over the last few years.

Chapter 6: Applying to a Radiography Program

There are some important things to consider during the application process to a radiography program. In order to be considered at the top of the list of program candidates, try to get straight "A's" in your prerequisite course work. This is a competitive field and every extra point counts. In extremely competitive programs, it is not uncommon to see the top 100 candidates having straight "A's" in their prerequisite courses.

So how does the school select the students if all of the top candidates have excellent grades? Here's where the extra mile comes in. If you already have a degree of some kind, most schools will look highly upon this. What they will look for next is experience in the health care field. If you have direct patient care experience, you will be considered above those without it. There are many ways to go about gaining that experience. Some schools recommend taking a phlebotomy, medical assisting, or a certified nursing assistant program prior to application. While these are beneficial, they do require an extra 6 months to a year of additional school prior to filing your application.

You may also consider applying for a patient transport job during prerequisite courses. They used to call them "runners." Now they call them "patient relocation specialists" or "patient logistics specialists". Basically, they bring patients on stretchers or wheelchairs to and from the radiology department. They have to learn CPR and how to properly transfer patients on and off the x-ray table. Today, most hospitals hire transporters for the entire facility and may probably not be solely working in the radiology department, but I would suggest that we still comprise the largest percentage of transportation jobs. In a radiology department, you can have good networking experiences, get to know x-ray techs, and get a feel for the work flow and duties of a radiologic technologist. Hospitals are more likely to promote internal employees rather than pay for extensive training of someone outside the hospital. It's a great place to start and you can always change jobs once you begin your program if your needs demand it. I'll discuss more on this later.

I would also like to recommend job shadowing prior to making the commitment to any radiography program. Shadowing has become more difficult due to patient privacy concerns and the HIPAA laws now in place (see Chapter 10: Legal Matters), but some have found ways to be compliant with the law and still offer this opportunity. I hate to admit it, but there are people who spend a few hours observing a radiologic technologist and ultimately decide it's not really something they really want to do. I learned after about two hours observing radiation therapy during a rotation in x-ray school that it simply wasn't for me. I applaud the individuals who commit themselves to that specialty and their service is greatly needed. It takes a special kind of person with the right affinity for patient care to be a good radiation therapist, but at that time in my life, I was nowhere near mature enough to work in that kind of environment. It was not the right fit for me at the time, but I'm thankful that I was given the opportunity to shadow and learn about that option within our field, and I gained a little bit of insight about myself.

In radiography programs I have taught for, I have heard several new students admit that they had no idea what they were getting themselves into. Radiographers do not simply push a button. You will see blood, body fluids, surgeries, feces, vomit, bones sticking out of the skin and additional unpleasant sights, while still being expected to obtain excellent x-rays despite these conditions. You will be around needles and be expected to provide quality care for patients. Please make sure you know what you're in for so you don't waste your time... the last thing you want to do is spend a couple of years getting through prerequisite courses and the application process only to find out that you aren't really interested in the field. This field is not for everyone, and it needs devoted individuals who are passionate about what they do.

Some x-ray programs may have an interview process as part of their screening for candidates. It is always good to brush up on interview techniques and professionalism, but it is not the purpose for this book to detail those attributes. Instead, here are some characteristics that educators look for in a radiography candidate:

They look for someone who is professional and well-groomed. If you walk in chewing gum and wearing jeans and a t-shirt with a risqué quote from a movie you once saw, chances are, you will not be found very presentable. No one on the interview committee will want you representing their institution to their hospital affiliates.

Don't be a "know-it-all." If your second cousin twice removed was a technologist, don't assume you know everything there is to know about becoming a technologist. Even if you *think* you do, it is not wise to express that during your interview. It *is* encouraged to admit that you understand that the requirements of an x-ray program require dedication and hard work, and you can promote your work ethic as being someone who can handle the load. Just make sure you're telling the truth.

Be flexible. Your clinical hours will require you to rotate to different departments, hospitals, and even different shifts. You need be able to align your personal schedule to accommodate whatever the clinical rotation requires in order to be successful.

The bottom line is you should have a good attitude. They are looking for people to be assertive, but not aggressive. They want to know that you will be proactive in your learning and that you are taking initiative while being teach-able at the same time. The technical skills can always be learned. They want to know that you are going to represent their institution well, take instruction to heart and get along with hospital staff that has been given the responsibility to teach you.

It is important to anyone reading this that I mention the declaration of any criminal record prior to starting an x-ray program. Most schools perform a background check, so they are likely to learn about your past anyway. But it is much more respectable to be upfront and disclose any past records that may arise once you apply for the ARRT exam. As part of your application process near the completion of school, you will be asked by the ARRT to disclose any history of convictions, misdemeanors, felonies, or military court martial. While some juvenile records and minor traffic violations are not required to be disclosed, anything involving drugs or alcohol, as well as any incidents of having a license revoked or suspended will be.

If you have something like this in your personal background, it doesn't necessarily mean that you will not be eligible to become a registered technologist. It does mean that you will need to have an ethics committee review. The sooner you disclose this information, the earlier on you will be able to begin this process, and save valuable time. It will look suspicious if none of this is disclosed early on in your program, and it just happens to become known as you approach your graduation date.

This also applies to any offenses that violate the honor code while you are in school prior to the completion of your program. This just goes to show that the ARRT is committed to the highest standards of ethics.

You may just find yourself in the middle of an ethics hearing if you make some mistakes, knowingly or not, during the course of your schooling. Driving under the influence will definitely draw some attention, especially if your license gets suspended or revoked. Diagnosing a radiograph will definitely land you in hot water. During school, you will be taught what lies within your scope as a radiographer, and what does not. Also, any violations of academic honesty policies are likely going to cause you to have a hearing. An example of a violation may be cheating on a test. Another example would be obtaining course material from a former student to use to memorize answers on your current curriculum. Plagiarism, or submitting someone else's work as your own, is also an issue that is taken very seriously.

It is more likely that students will have situations that need to be mentioned from before entrance into a radiography program, but occasionally things happen while in school as well. Most students don't realize the implications of their actions until it's too late, so it's a good idea to familiarize yourself with the expectations that will be placed upon you. You can read more about the ARRT Standards of Ethics here: https://www.arrt.org/pdfs/Governing-Documents/Standards-of-Ethics.pdf

Part II: During School

Chapter 7: What to Expect in your Classes

I have witnessed many students drop out of a radiography program before mid-terms in their first semester for two reasons that can easily be avoided. The first is because proper investigation may not have been conducted on the student's behalf about the field. Hopefully, the first two chapters of this book will be enough of an influence to spread the word to the community that some level of research needs to be done. The second reason is simply because they did not have a realistic expectation of the kind of commitment that is required for classes, studying and clinical rotations.

I know that sounds like a negative way to go about promoting my field through this book, but it is the unfortunate truth, and it is something that all educators are disappointed to see. Students sometimes speculate that the first two semesters of any program are designed to "weed people out." That assumption usually disappears around the middle of the third or fourth semester (beyond the half-way point) when the content of the curriculum can become even more challenging. The concepts do not necessarily become more difficult, but you are beginning to combine a multitude of concepts already learned in the first few semesters and you're expected to place them into practice. The schools do not want to see you fail, and frankly, it is not in their best interest. Whether private or public, a radiography program has nothing to gain by reducing the number of seats filled in its classrooms. For these reasons, your complete investment in the program is necessary before making the commitment to undergo a rigorous training program such as radiography.

During most program information sessions, as well as in day-one orientation, it doesn't matter how many times the speaker will emphasize the time commitment involved, I guarantee you that course work in a two-year radiography program is more intensive than any other general education courses you have experienced thus far. I'm not trying to deter you from this field, but rather to realistically inform you so that you are not set up to fail.

My experience during school was very similar to every x-ray program that I have had the privilege to teach for. My first semester was filled by 12 units of introductory courses in our program. A good rule of thumb to get an idea about how much study time is needed for classes, assume that each hour of in-class instruction that you receive should be supplemented by two hours of studying per week. For me in that first semester, that equaled about 24 hours of studying. On top of that, I did a clinical rotation for 16 hours per week (usually it was Tuesdays and Thursdays for eight hours each). Add it all up, and that was approximately 52 hours per week plus time to commute, eat, and... oh yeah, work so I could pay the bills. Being fresh out of high school, I had the youth and energy to work nearly full-time during the duration of my training, but ended up moving back in with my parents at some point prior to graduation. Not everyone has that option though. There were people that could pull off working full-time, supporting themselves and their families, and succeeding in school but I imagine they may have needed a month or two of relaxation after taking their final exams due to exhaustion.

As a radiography student you have to quickly learn how to optimize your time in the beginning, and the earlier this happens, the better. I was 19 years old when I entered my x-ray program and had been working part-time building personal computers for a small, family owned store. It was decent money at the time, but my job was not flexible enough to maintain the schedule that my radiography program demanded. I had to let that job go, and find one that was suitable to my needs in a hurry because the second semester of my program involved 40 hours of clinic per week followed by night classes. Some friends working for the city put a good word in for me at the local community center. I interviewed, and was hired to work as a "recreation leader" during the evenings and on weekends. What this meant was basically this; I arrived at work at 5:00 p.m. on my week nights, and had an array of shifts to choose from on the weekends. I would sit at the front desk of the community center or the senior citizens center and welcome guests. I had the freedom to study as long as I still met the needs of anyone renting out one of the rooms. I would get up once every hour or so to check on the guests, maybe exchange trash bags that were getting full, or to just stretch my legs (note: taking a break from studying every 45 minutes or so will help your concentration). Usually, the last two hours from about 11:00 p.m. to 1:00 a.m. was closing time. I would make sure everyone was out of the building, and then I cleaned the floors, tables, chairs and restrooms. Then I would rearrange the tables and chairs into a pre-determined configuration so that the morning staff could simply open the doors and let guests in.

This wasn't glorious work by any means, but it allowed me to earn a pay check while I studied for 75% of my shift. If you are like most people that need to work while you go to school, it may be worth the pay cut it took (whatever cut you can manage and still meet your day to day needs) in order to trade off for a job that allows you to study while being paid. Some students have told me they have had similar jobs like night security, limousine driver, or gas station attendant. The point is, if you absolutely must work during school, and if you can study while getting paid, you're setting yourself up for successful time-management for the next two years.

I was fortunate enough to complete my program at a young age, but many students (especially in this economy) are doing this as a second, or possibly a third career. Most x-ray programs I have seen are extremely diverse. There are students of all nationalities, ages, and professional backgrounds. If you are married or have children in the house, a radiography program is not impossible, but you need to make sure that you have a good support system in place with realistic expectations. Having some money in savings will be essential and having people to lean on when school demands so much of your time and energy is a necessity. There are going to be unforeseen circumstances in anyone's life that will prevent perfect attendance, so make sure that you know up front what your school's attendance policy is and keep it in mind when weighing the need to take time off.

Chapter 8: Skills Needed for Success

I often visit online forums in the radiography world, and one of the more popular topics for discussion is the types of skills that are required to perform the job of a radiologic technologist. One thing that I will usually recommend is to go online to any hospital's human resources page and look at the job postings. There will be a basic job description that may shed some light for you. If there's something on that description that you don't know how to do, that's okay. School will train you to be competent at everything you see on the page. What you need to be looking for are things that you know you *do not* want to do, and decide if this is a career direction you would still like to pursue.

Physically speaking, you will need to be able to demonstrate proper body mechanics and lift about 50 lbs per the standard job description. Your program will teach you the proper methods for transferring patients to and from stretchers, wheelchairs, and the x-ray table. You will also be performing regular repetitive motion with some fairly heavy equipment in the x-ray department. Our portable fluoroscopic equipment can be quite heavy, as well as a portable x-ray machine, but these are typically power-assisted.   Portable exams are the types of activities that will stress your body physically more than most procedures for x-ray techs. These will require placing a large (14″ x 17″) image receptor weighing sometimes up to 10 or 12 lbs. underneath a patient who is lying on a soft bed. There are many tips and tricks that one can learn to get the image receptors in position, but even with the best methods out there, expect to be sweating after 5 or 6 in a row. You should also be able to be on your feet for most of the day. In a busy radiology department, you may not sit down except for when you are on a break, and in some states, you may not be guaranteed a break at any specific time, or at all.

As far as educational background goes, your prerequisite courses are vital, as your studies will depend on mastery of subjects like medical terminology, anatomy and physiology, English and math. A basic knowledge of the order of operations in algebra will be important as well. The curriculum has plenty of math problems for you to solve in algebraic "find the value of x" format. You will need to rely on your instruction to find out which formulas are used for which situations, but as long as you know how to solve a problem algebraically, you should be in fairly good standing.

As previously stated, being well-organized is going to help you out a lot. If you're not typically the "organized" type of person, you can still manage well enough, but learning how to build your organizational skills will help you in the long run. Being able to take notes quickly and more importantly, being able to refer back to them when you have a limited amount of time to study will prove to help greatly. Reading your material ahead of time will also prevent you from feeling overwhelmed during lecture when topics are covered quickly. And good communication is essential; with your instructors, fellow classmates, the staff techs at your clinical rotation, and the patients you will encounter. Interpersonal communication cannot be something implied or assumed in this kind of setting. It needs to be precise, straight-forward, and often empathetic.

Being out of your comfort zone is something that you will need to get used to. This may not qualify as a traditional skill, but a type of mind set that you should learn to approach the clinical environment with. You can practice patient positioning and manipulating the x-ray equipment all day long on a classmate or a willing family member, but that first time you perform an exam on a patient will be a bit uncomfortable. Keep in mind during lecture that you should be developing the ability to retain what you have learned in class and be able to appropriately apply the concept in the hospital setting with real patients. A general knowledge of the fact that the best way to learn and improve is to perform exams as opposed to practicing them will ensure that you have a realistic expectation of what the experience will be like. The comfort zone gradually creeps closer throughout your education, but that first semester can mimic the feeling one has when learning how to drive with other motorists on the street (I taught myself on a manual transmission – not a pretty sight). Assertiveness will gain you a lot of respect in this environment. Remember, everyone working at the hospital has been in your shoes and understands how you will be feeling. It takes courage to step out of that comfort zone, but the sooner you do the better when it comes to clinical practice. Get used to saying "let me try that."

Willingness to go the extra mile; this is important in about every aspect of the phrase that I can think of. When interacting with patients, treat them all as if they are a close family member. If someone in the hallway needs directions, don't simply point in the direction that they need to go, but instead walk them there. If extra credit is offered in your course work, do it even if you are already making 100% in the class. If you have never taken any college courses, you need to know that you will be held responsible for anything discussed in class, included in the assigned reading material, and for any tests and/or quizzes missed because you are tardy or absent in most programs. Make sure you know the grading scale, which may be different from the traditional scale in most classes. I had to score 95% to get an A in my program, and I have made it routine practice to use anywhere between 90% and 93% in order to obtain an A in the courses I teach.

It is difficult to know what to expect in such foreign territory, but you will have an orientation or information session that should explain a lot. It will probably be a bit overwhelming at first, and you may find yourself in a room full of your classmates-to-be who will not ask many questions in the beginning, but once someone breaks the ice, the questions tend to fly. The orientation is your opportunity to clarify any expectations that are still vague. There will always be some variation between x-ray programs, but you should leave your orientation session with a good idea of what to expect. Don't be afraid to ask any question because there may be many students in the room who are wondering the same thing you are, but who may not be willing to speak up in a group setting just yet. Remember... be assertive. The information session will provide a lot of answers about what to expect from your program, and also about what the program is expecting from you.

Chapter 9: The Clinical Assignment

The hospital setting is like no other setting I have experienced. You may find yourself amongst medical personnel of varying experience and educational levels. Along with radiography students, there will also be students in other specialties like nursing, respiratory therapy, phlebotomy, surgical tech, and medical assisting. Each field will have its own set of challenges, but one thing is true of all clinical learning; there are many ways to perform a task. I will continue to reemphasize this concept throughout this book.

When you first set foot in the radiology department, you will see busy technologists running around performing their duties and making it look easy. You might also see second year students from your own or other schools, but it may be difficult to distinguish them from hospital employees at first. After some department and hospital orientation, a tour, and hopefully some introductions to staff, you will most likely be assigned to stick with a seasoned technologist. Each technologist may have a differing theory about what kind of student learning should take place. Before discussing each method in detail, just remember that everyone learns differently and all students will end up in the same place at the end of their perspective programs.

These technologists know that the first day you step into their environment, you may not have learned the theory behind x-ray beam production or how to properly position a patient for every single exam. It's going to take you two years to learn everything you need to know, and a large portion of it will be in the classroom. It is their job to show you how to perform exams (under their supervision) without having that official knowledge. Some techs are excellent at thoroughly explaining everything just as if you were in a class, some expect you to learn by observation, and quite often, there isn't a lot of time in a fully-functioning radiology department for anyone to step aside and have a 10 minute mini-lecture about every single procedure that occurs in your exam room. The reality is that you will learn no matter what level of "formal" instruction is given, and you should try to be as observant as possible. Most technologists will not have any background in education, but if you are attentive to detail, you will be able to pick up some handy tricks that a seasoned veteran will employ which may not be covered in your textbook. And make a point to share with your class also. You are in this together.

The hospital's techs know you need basic instruction in the beginning. It's your duty to show them that you can be professional, courteous, and willing to learn. Interpersonal skills are important in the patient care setting. One moment, you will be interacting with a patient who is in pain, and the next patient will be extremely upset about something. Some patients experience loss during their stay in the hospital, and some may not have had any visitors for a few days. They may not have even left their room and they're yearning for an open ear during the time they are in your exam room. Sometimes a listening ear can often be therapeutic, and can go a long way when we are focused on providing the best patient care at all times.

In addition to patient interaction, you may be working with different technologists with their own stress. You will certainly encounter many dynamic personalities in the clinical setting and will need to be able to work alongside of technologists regardless of your differences. When two people are under stress, these differences can become more pronounced. Can you get along with staff? How do you interact with patients who are intoxicated, irate, and combative, in pain, depressed or non-responsive? Whether it is the technologist you are directly working with or someone else, there will always be someone observing you in these situations. Remember that you will eventually want to work after you graduate... this truly is a 2-year job interview.

Chapter 10: Legal Matters

Your school will prepare you for the legalities that you will need to be aware of. Laws vary by state, and it would be difficult for me to write a chapter that encompasses all of that information. There will be some differences based on where you are that you should educate yourselves about if you plan on relocating. Your school will prepare you in great detail for the requirements in your specific region, but without much prior classroom instruction before your initial clinical experience, here are a few things that are extremely important to consider when training in the United States.

The number one patient safety initiative by the Joint Commission on Accreditation of Healthcare Organizations (http://www.jointcommission.org/) is proper identification of patients. You will learn within your curriculum about the history of lawsuits that have occurred in our country concerning surgical procedures, patient examinations and medical treatment that has been performed on the wrong patient. First and foremost, prior to doing any exam on any patient is that you ensure proper identification of the patient. Your hospital should go through this during orientation, but JCAHO requires two patient identifiers, and it never hurts to perform three. You should be checking the patient's armband, comparing it with you paperwork, and verbally confirming the patient's full name, date of birth, and/or medical record number.

Another important guideline to remember is that as a radiography student, you must be under the direct or indirect supervision of a registered technologist. Direct supervision means that the tech is with you, by your side, in the same exam room while you position and expose your patient to radiation. Indirect supervision will come a little later after you have been deemed competent in performing some procedures. Indirect supervision means that you may perform an exam with a technologist nearby. That means that you can verbally call out for help, and the technologist (who cannot be caring for another patient) can freely come in the room to help you at the time of your request. You will not be permitted to perform examinations without a technologist present. It is both the hospital's and the school's responsibility that there is one technologist assigned to work with each student in a 1:1 ratio.

The Health Insurance Portability and Accountability Act (HIPAA) was originated in 1996 and was created to protect patient privacy. Your x-ray program will prepare you to protect patient privacy, as should your hospital, which will have its own policy for you to review. Bottom line, HIPAA requirements keep you from sharing confidential patient information with anyone who is not directly involved in the patient's exam. Many lawsuits occur each year as a result of HIPAA violations. To learn more about HIPAA, visit the U.S. Department of Health and Human Services Department's website at http://www.hhs.gov/ocr/privacy/hipaa/understanding/index.html.

Procedure consent forms are completed by physicians, RN's and technologists. They are more formally known as "informed consent" and should not be signed by students. During any invasive procedures or exams that require a contrast injection that you may encounter later in your x-ray program, patients fill out a separate form with a series of questions that will inform the physician if there are any contraindications (reasons the procedure might be harmful to the patient). The physician then explains the procedure to the patient, as well as the risks, benefits and possible alternatives. It is up to the patient, who has the right to refuse any procedure, if he or she wants to continue with the proposed exam or treatment. Once the patient and physician agree to proceed, both sign the consent form and staff begins any physical preparation for the patient.

You may also encounter a physician who instructs a student to perform exams, or additional exams on a patient. If this is not written down by the physician at the time, it is considered a "verbal order". Verbal orders can be legally accepted by RN's and radiologic technologists, but not by students. It is important to acquire the order in writing or bring someone qualified to receive verbal orders in order to proceed with the request. Again, your program will explain this in greater detail, but possibly after you begin your clinical rotation.

Another legal issue that you may witness has to do with proper operation of fluoroscopic equipment, or live (real time) x-rays. Laws and guidelines vary from state to state regarding who is qualified to operate fluoro and under what circumstances. For instance, I worked in North Carolina for about four years, and there were no state regulations on radiation protection. Literally anyone could perform radiographic exams or operate a fluoroscope. California, where I live now and where I received my initial training, is very strict in the regulation of who can and cannot operate a fluoroscope. Only a physician with a state fluoroscopic permit or supervisor/operator permit may operate a fluoroscope, and a technologist who has a permit can under the supervision of a physician with a supervisor/operator license or permit. It is important to find out what your state guidelines are, and that you are abiding by them at all times. Your instructors should be able to answer this question for you right away.

This may seem like an odd section to include in this book, but I am including it for a very good reason. Like I said, your curriculum will train you how to properly abide by all of these legalities, but the technologists training you are human. As with any human, there are some who uphold the highest of ethical standards, as well as some who find some of these guidelines to possess gray areas. It is unfortunate that some will bend the rules or let some of these things slide in certain circumstances, but it is absolutely imperative that you do not. Making a wrong decision at this stage of your education could put patient safety, your career, the hospital's reputation, and the school's learning contract with that hospital at risk. The supervising technologist may have their x-ray license/registration revoked for allowing this, and/or you may be found ineligible to receive one if caught doing something that you are not yet qualified to do.

Chapter 11: Professionalism in Health Care

Making a good first impression to your clinical site can prove to be advantageous later. Someone once told me "there's no second chance to make a good first impression." It sounds rather cliché, but it's mostly true. To anyone who has worked in the professional world, this chapter may seem like common sense, but even still, there may be some new expectations about professionalism that might not have occurred to you regarding working in the medical field that will be worth reading.

Good professional conduct will keep you out of trouble and promote the belief that you are someone who follows rules and understands their purpose. Professional language without profanity is highly overlooked. You may think you are having a private conversation with a technologist who makes a habit of using profanity at work, but there are very few private areas in a hospital. It is quite possible someone can overhear just about anything you say.

Keep personal contact to a minimum. You have to touch patients as part of your job, but you can explain what you're doing and do so appropriately without causing alarm. There should be no reason to touch a technologist or a fellow student. It doesn't matter how far you go back with your classmate, giving them a shoulder massage in the clinical setting is inappropriate, even if it is welcomed by the participant. It can be *perceived* as inappropriate by hospital staff or patients and should be avoided. Eating, drinking and chewing gum are not permitted in patient care areas. It seems common for a hospital to be lenient on some of these things, but it is a JCAHO standard that should be abided by, and only covered drinks can be kept in a non-patient care area while at work. Lunch and all other food and drink should be kept in the designated break room.

Whether you realize it or not, people who don't know you will judge you by your appearance. Patients don't know you, but your appearance is the first thing they will notice about you. Make sure that your hair is neatly groomed and fingernails trimmed to prevent bacteria from collecting underneath your nails (infection control standard). Piercings should be removed according to hospital policy, as well as tattoos being covered. I have had to counsel several students about appearance and body odor in the past. Make sure to bathe daily and that you do not sleep in your scrubs and wear them into clinic. Although I do admit, they are comfortable enough to sleep in.

Also, be sensitive about how much cologne or perfume you wear. You may be treating patients who are nauseated or possibly undergoing chemotherapy. These patients will have a heightened sensitivity to odors, and it could make them feel worse if you dunk yourself in your favorite Friday night scent. Wearing anything fragrant is typically not advised.

We have discussed attitude already, but in addition to it, you may encounter technologists who perform different exams in different ways than you learned in class. There are multiple ways to do just about any exam, and you may learn something new or decide to adopt a new method of performing an exam yourself by observing a variety of methods. The worst thing you can do when you observe a different way to perform a procedure is tell a technologist that they are doing it all wrong. It will not accomplish anything in your favor, and will only serve to give that tech a good reason to avoid working with you.

Remember, they are making extra effort to train you with skills they have picked up in their experience and their goal is to promote independent performance by you. How receptive you are to what they are trying to show you will directly influence their quality of instruction. Although they are working at a hospital that is a teaching institution, they don't have to go above and beyond to provide extra information to you. Their first priority is the patient, and your education is, and should be, secondary to patient care.

On occasion, you may encounter a technologist doing something in a manner that is unsafe or inappropriate. This is where you must become tactful in how you approach the problem. For most of these situations (as long as it is not harmful in any way), treat them as examples of what NOT to do. Any instance that jeopardizes patient safety should be dealt with delicately. For instance, I once heard about a tech who never provided gonadal shielding for his patients, a practice everyone taught from day one in school to protect the reproductive organs (some of the most sensitive tissue to radiation in the body). The student soon told me about this. As the clinical instructor, I instructed the student to ask the technologist if the students could start applying shielding to the patient before each exposure was made in order to "start getting into a good habit" as suggested by the clinical instructor. This was beneficial because the patient received the appropriate radiation protection, and the technologist didn't become defensive or perceive the student's suggestion as accusatory.

The tech was very receptive to this, and began doing it more regularly themselves as a result. What do you think the results would have been if the student bluntly told the tech, "You're not shielding your patients."? It would not have gone over very well. If you are having trouble approaching situations like this tactfully, make sure to ask your clinical instructor or one of your teachers about it.

It doesn't happen often, but it does occur occasionally that a technologist refuses to perform in a manner that is required of them. At this point, it's time to go up the chain of command. You don't want to put yourself in the middle of disciplinary action between the technologist and their employer. You may not want to be a "rat" by saying anything, but if a patient gets injured by a neglect in performance of duties by a technologist and it is later known that you were aware of the behavior and did not say anything, you might share some liability for those injuries and be held responsible even though you weren't doing it yourself.

Fraternization with hospital staff is usually very innocent, but can potentially be devastating to your career if handled inappropriately. I would avoid this as much as possible while you are a student. There should be a bold line distinguishing the role of the clinical affiliate technologist and the student. The student is there to learn from the employed tech and should learn as much as possible that is work-related. I like to think of this relationship as being similar to the supervisor/employee relationship, even though you are not directly employed by the technologist or hospital (yet). It is very easy to become relaxed in setting where you believe you are among friends and professionalism can decline quickly when one's guard is down. If a technologist asks you to go to a party after your clinical rotation on a Friday night, ask yourself, "would this be appropriate if I were employed by this person?" If the party is a Christmas party where all staff and students have been invited, you are more than likely on the safe side as long as you still practice good behavior. If you are the only student invited and the technologist inviting you is the only representative from the hospital, you may be setting yourself up for disaster in this inappropriate scenario.

Any good warning on fraternization should be accompanied by the discouragement of dating a fellow student, and especially, a hospital employee. You may hear music from the heavens every time a certain someone enters the room, and you may feel like this person is "the one," but be warned... entering a relationship with a fellow classmate or staff tech while in school is a risk to all of your hard work and effort. Is this risk worth the price you may pay for taking it? You may think that you (and your potential boyfriends/girlfriends) are mature enough to avoid allowing a small disagreement or argument from influencing your performance... until one of you has your reputation on the line. There is a good chance that at least one of you would make a good candidate for the Jerry Springer show under this circumstance.

I have seen my share of disputes about inappropriate fraternization of students. Ultimately the school or the hospital cannot decide or mandate what you do in your free time, but they have the responsibility of holding you accountable for your performance while in the classroom or hospital setting. I have seen a lot of people become very uncomfortable when relationships go wrong in both professional and academic settings. There is a good reason why a dating policy exists in so many places of employment. Many hospitals even have policies that prohibit spouses from being employed in the same department. Make sure you check the school's policies on fraternization and dating, and know them well.

Chapter 12: Social Media

One of the more recent battlegrounds for similar issues is fought in the digital realm. You may have even learned about this book through referral from one of your friends or on a social media site. For advertising, social media has become quite influential and a great tool for someone like me, looking to get the word out about how to succeed through x-ray school. However, social media has added a new, more complex set of problems to deal with concerning fraternization, HIPAA, and behavioral issues.

When considering "friending" people from school or the hospital on social media sites, you may want to consider avoiding it altogether. If you absolutely cannot avoid it, consider creating a separate identity for professional contacts. You don't want one of your old high school buddies mooning you on a picture posted to your site for all your new professional contacts to see. You should also act professionally here as well. If people are connected to you through professional sources, think about how many other contacts might be viewing every word you say or picture you post. Your name will become associated with that content, and you may find yourself having made a bad impression before you are even granted an interview for a job in the future because of it. My last three employers have admitted to "googling" me prior to arranging an interview for a position. You should try this now. Put this book down and "google" yourself. Just type your name into the search bar at www.google.com. Did you find anything that would make a bad impression for a potential employer? You might want to take care of this yesterday. Check your privacy settings on sites that have information that you might consider personal or unprofessional if a potential employer may get a glance at it. Remember, "There's no second chance to make a good first impression."

As far as HIPAA is concerned, it seems obvious that you should not post any patient information or stories pertaining to patients onto Facebook, Twitter, etc. It is also not appropriate to make derogatory comments about patients, staff or classmates in this fashion. People visit the hospital in confidence that their information will be kept private, and many lawsuits have been filed for violation of HIPAA law. This is the time for you to earn the trust of patients and hospital staff and not to take it lightly. Just remember, a lot of the social media sites do not offer the option to retract information that is published. Think at least three times before posting anything, and it never hurts to ask "would my mother want this information made public about her?"

If you have read my blog (http://bloggingradiography.blogspot.com), you may notice that I have several actual x-rays of patients posted there. What you will never see on those x-rays is information about who the patient is or where the exam was performed. In fact, I receive many x-ray submissions from people who read my blog that I have no idea where or when the x-rays were taken. I would not suggest that you post x-ray examinations to social media sites at all when you are a student, but you may be asked to collect images for purposes related to classroom discussion or assignments. Your instructors will do so after you are given explicit detail about what information can and cannot be on an x-ray examination prior to it leaving the confines of the hospital, and certain hospitals may not allow this at all, even if all identifiable information is removed. Once you have moved on past radiography school and have been properly trained and have attained appropriate permission, then you can consider doing something like a blog. If you end up doing that, please shoot me an email and I would be happy to collaborate with you, but until then, protect yourself and don't do anything foolish.

Chapter 13: Becoming Competent in your Procedures

Right off the bat you will be asked to observe clinical procedures on actual patients. Many times, this occurs on examinations that you have not yet had formal classroom instruction for. This can be a double-edged sword. One of the first exams that you will learn, and the most performed radiographic examination, is the chest x-ray. Your classroom and lab instructor may demonstrate how to perform this once or twice before moving onto the next topic, but you will most likely see this demonstrated in your clinical site hundreds of times during your first week. The challenge is in remembering the properly demonstrated method from class while detecting inconsistencies in practice in the actual clinical setting. A technologist may forget to shield or restrict the x-ray beam in a hurry where as your instructor may emphasize the importance of these things during the lengthy presentation. Devoting all of your attention, taking good notes, and reviewing your notes will serve to implant good practices in your mind.

Once you have studied a particular procedure in class and you have studied your notes profusely, it's going to be obvious that not every single tech out there performs a procedure the same way your instructor taught you. They will most likely get the job done, but what kind of job? Do these techs routinely submit sub-par work or submit images with sloppy presentation? This is when you need to ask yourself, "What kind of tech do I want to be?"

There is an appropriate balance between quality and quantity regarding many things in your x-ray program. You have to be able to find that balance that works for you to produce images of excellent quality while maintaining a certain level of efficiency. The efficiency will come later after much practice. But practice is the key... if you practice how to quickly perform a lumbar spine series without ever fine-tuning the position of the central ray and your collimation, you will probably become the tech that gets things done in a hurry, but your coworkers might not necessarily want you to perform exams on their children due to the excess radiation exposure. If you take too much time to perfect every aspect of each exposure, you will struggle in emergency situations like trauma and surgery. You will not be expected to excel in both areas in the beginning, but as you get closer to your graduation date, you will find yourself improving in both areas (realistically one more than the other). You just need to keep this in mind when you're a student so that you make appropriate progress. It can also be helpful to determine what kind of setting you would like to work in when you graduate.

When you think of the term "initiative", what does it mean to you? Hopefully, it's something like this: "The power or ability to begin or follow through energetically with a plan or task." It also means becoming *comfortable* with being *uncomfortable,* as stated before.

A couple of months prior to graduating from my x-ray program, I was enticed to try snowboarding for the first time (as a side note, you should avoid learning a new extreme sport while in school). Nevertheless, I spent half of the day barely moving down the hill, scared, frustrated and trying not to fall. My friend and self-proclaimed snowboarding instructor, who was not present for any of this except for my embarrassing dismount fail from the lift chair my first time up the slope that morning, told me something very motivating when we regrouped for lunch. After explaining my frustrations with the learning process, he told me in his infinite wisdom, "Dude, if you're not falling, you're not trying hard enough."

I was at first annoyed with this statement until I arrived at the top of the mountain again. Thinking about it more in depth, my mode of thought changed from simply just avoiding a fall to focusing on learning how to turn and how to stop. That required momentum. Once I got that down, I learned how to turn the opposite direction. I even figured out how to dismount the lift without falling by early afternoon. He was absolutely right. There was a transformation of thought that occurred which told me that my focus was all wrong at all in the beginning. There was less risk the way I had gone about learning to snowboard before lunch. Of course, it hurt worse the faster I went after lunch, but I fell far less with my new outlook. It was more uncomfortable, but I got used to that feeling and at the end of the day, I didn't want to leave. My friend took a nap in the car while I went down the slope a few more times.

As with any skill, it is important to continue to develop confidence in what you have learned. Confidence requires a certain balance... too little confidence and you may have a real challenge with your rate of progression with any skill. Too much confidence can sometimes turn into cockiness. If you get cocky, there will always be someone to knock you right back down into place, and it just might take a while to rebuild some of that confidence depending on how that is accomplished. I'll give you an example of each scenario.

When I first got accepted into my radiography program, I was required to go through lab testing and vaccinations that was all offered by the school. In the office of the nursing department, I encountered a nurse (not a student, but most likely a new grad) that lacked confidence in her ability to draw blood. I have always been more of a quiet observer type of person, and was so especially prior to the completion of my x-ray schooling. I watched this nurse carefully prep the supplies for drawing blood, which she did efficiently and confidently. It was obvious that she knew what to do and that she had much practice. However, when she put on her gloves, picked up the needle, and turned toward me, something shifted in her body language. Our eyes met and she looked like she had seen a ghost. I looked down to observe her hand holding the needle, and it was trembling. I don't mean trembling like one gets the jitters after drinking too much coffee, but really trembling like she was going to slice my arm open if she got near me with that needle.

Knowing that she was the only nurse in the place and I wasn't going to get out of there without this woman placing a needle in my vein, I decided to try to make her feel more at ease. After all, I would soon be in similar shoes and will probably be experiencing my own nervous behavior. I told her that I was recently accepted to the radiography program, and that I was going to be required to learn how to do I.V. sticks myself. I asked her to walk me through the steps, which I was sure she knew considering her display of skill up to this point, hoping it would take her mind off of whatever it was that was making her nervous. After all, she had been trusted by the school to operate solo in this office. Someone must have had confidence in her skills. Once she began thinking about each step she had learned and began reciting them to me, she seemed more relaxed, and she stopped her trembling (thank goodness).

Just from a simple observation, I could tell that she was well versed in technique, but for some reason she lacked confidence. I've always wondered what was going through that nurse's mind when she was trembling. She may have had a bad experience herself with I.V.'s or she may have been considering what her patient was thinking about her skills... who knows? What I do know is that she did an excellent job once her concentration was focused on her skill set, but she needed a little reassurance, which in my opinion she gave herself once she got her mind off of whatever she was thinking about that made her tremble. Mostly, when this happens, it is not because a lack of knowledge exists, but lack of practice. The more you practice a skill, the quicker it becomes second-nature and you can build so much confidence that you begin to do it automatically without even thinking about the step-by-step routine which you once read about in a text book.

The opposite problem, having too much confidence, can be even more of a detriment to one's reputation. I remember the rants and raves of a technologist who contributed to my training that used to walk around and tell everyone in the hospital in Muhammad Ali fashion, "I am the greatest x-ray tech of all tiiiiiiiiime!" "Aint nobody in the world shootin as many films without repeats as me!" I could honestly say that about 99% of the time, he was right. He had great technical skills.

During one of my operating room rotations, this technologist allowed me to perform the operation of the c-arm under his observation. I was having difficulty obtaining a particular oblique view without my image intensifier colliding with some of the instruments when he decided to step in and take over. Normally when he took over an exam, it meant that this particular tech would not allow me to put me hands on anything else for the rest of the day, and he would use the situation as an opportunity to belittle the students or initiate bragging about his own skills. This time, he did both with his monologue. He said, "Man, don't you rookies ever listen to what I say? You're not even a rookie... you're just going to school trying to be a rookie. You need to listen..." During his monologue he had been looking at me while taking over control of the c-arm and placing it into the position that the doctor wanted. He did not notice that he bumped a retractor – a device used to hold the tissue open around the spine during this procedure, and it had shifted in the patient.

This is exactly what I had been attempting to avoid. It didn't hurt the patient, but the doctor got really upset. He grabbed the c-arm so it couldn't be moved, which made the technologist turn to look at him, pointed a finger at the tech, and sternly said, "You... Get out of my O.R." The technologist looked humiliated. He looked at me and said "come on, Jeremy." Before I had a chance to react, the doctor said, "Leave the kid... but you can go." The tech looked at the ground and walked out. As a side-note I wasn't supposed to be operating a c-arm without supervision as a student, so I had to call our department to get another technologist in the room with me.

Apparently, this technologist thought he could do his job without even looking. He was wrong. It took everything for me not to feel cocky after the doctor requested that I stay and that my skills were being preferred over the tech's with all the experience. The doctor, knowing I was a student, told me that if his instruments were ever getting in the way of my c-arm and I couldn't work around them, I should speak up so he could move something. He also said he didn't need "cocky people" on his surgical team. It's alright to feel good about a compliment, but the same thing can happen to anyone who gets cocky... try to remain humble.

Chapter 14: Developing a Plan

By now, you will be well underway with your program by this point, and you will be surprised at how fast time flies up to this point. The least stressful time in any academic program is at the beginning of a semester (prior to diving into the first week's lessons). If you had any kind of break prior to your new classes starting this is when you can relax, unwind, and start thinking about where you want to be in 5 years. You might be thinking, "I just want to make it through this program." But trust me, when I discuss interviewing for jobs later in this book, you will be thankful you will have already been thinking about this long ahead.

If you have made it through the first entire year, you should congratulate yourself. Most people who begin the second year complete the program. People who didn't make it this far are usually spread too thin with the time commitment that the program requires, and have multiple responsibilities, possibly a family, job, and I have even seen unforeseen circumstances prevent completion of a program like illness or car accidents. Of course, there are a few who need additional tutoring and to possibly repeat a course before they can consider their program completed. Once you start the second year, regardless of how long it took you to get to this point, you will be gaining valuable experience at an exponential rate.

I have to be honest when I say that the expectations placed on you, especially in clinical rotations, will be increased. You will be expected to perform a lot of exams independently, although under indirect supervision. Your efficiency will be greater than that of the newly entering class of first-year students. To them, you will be somewhat indistinguishable from the technologists who work at the facility you are rotating through. I love to see the faces of the first year students when I have introduced second year students to them. They can't believe that after one year, you are already operating the equipment, speaking with ease to patients, and undertaking so much responsibility with, to what looks to them like, so little effort. Whether you realize it or not, your role has changed now to include mentor. And trust me when I say that if you are not doing something by the book, a first year who observes this will discuss it in their positioning class with your instructor and all of the first-year students. You still need to have you're a-game.

During the second year, you will find yourself more comfortable in clinic, and you will move to more advanced topics in your classes. Use this time to fine-tune clinical skills and network. Remember when I said that the x-ray program is like a two-year job interview? Thus far, the technologists at your clinical rotations have made some judgments about you and will be starting to decide if you might or might not be a good fit within their department. A lot of opinions will have been based on your personality and ability to interact with staff techs and patients. In year two, these judgments will shift a bit. Everyone knows you will not be functioning quite as independently as a staff tech, but they will be interacting with you and wondering "Is this someone I would want to work with?" Do you take initiative to perform exams or do you leave the less desirable exams (for whatever reason) for someone else to do. Do you volunteer to help other technologists when you are otherwise unoccupied by a patient exam? Jobs everywhere are full of people that want to clock in, do as little work as possible, and then clock out without contributing very much to any sort of team effort. Let this question guide your actions in clinic: "Who would these technologists prefer to be on their team?"

You should be starting to develop a strategy on finding employment or continuing school to an advanced modality. You don't need anything set in stone at this point, but try to keep an open mind. Most programs leave the special rotations into other areas of the radiology department for the second year. Some require you to go everywhere, while other programs will only allow you to choose one or two. Before you are asked where you would like to go, put some thought into it. Special rotations might include, but are not limited to the night or weekend shifts, the operating room, trauma bay, DEXA scanning, mammography, ultrasound, computed tomography, MRI, nuclear medicine, radiation therapy, cardiac cath lab, interventional radiography, or possibly PET (positron emission tomography).

First things first though. You need to finish your required x-ray work. Focus on finishing the required competencies early in your final semester. Your program should prioritize meeting the requirements of the radiography program prior to letting you rotate, so make sure you give yourself plenty of time to explore your future career possibilities and to meet and interact with those currently performing those jobs.

Another strategy you might start to consider at the beginning of your second year is to begin reviewing some of your prior course work that you may have forgotten. This will aide in your final semester, even though you will have a capstone course designed for review. Most of your peers will have long forgotten all of the specifics of measurements, tube angulations, and math formulas.

Chapter 15: Selecting a Special Rotation

During your second year, you will be given an opportunity to rotate through one or multiple advanced modalities in the radiology department. Regardless of which special rotation you eventually select, the strategy here is the same: Network, network, and network. Sometimes you may be asked to travel to a different hospital or clinical site to observe an advanced modality and I have heard a lot of students complain about this. Usually it's because a student becomes comfortable with the staff they are around every day and nobody likes to be the "new guy" in any environment. Going somewhere completely different can work in your favor, especially if you graduate, and the hospital you trained at is not hiring. Now is the time to extend your reach beyond what is comfortable, and chances are, the technologists at the hospital you are traveling to will know most of the people at the hospital you came from, and can get some inside information about your work ethic if they really want to. The world of radiography is small, and you would be surprised who knows who in the community. Try to make a good impression, and if you are really interested in the modality you came to observe, ask if you can keep in contact with some of the technologists you encounter or to use them as a reference when you apply for advanced modality training. You never know who will be hiring for a position when you're ready for a job, but the more people you meet and interact with, the more job opportunities you can find out about through word of mouth, which can often be faster than the ability of a Human Resources department to publically post a position.

If you're reading this book prior to beginning your x-ray program, or even in the first year, you might not be very familiar with the varying modalities and what they do. I'll try to briefly summarize them:

DEXA scanning stands for "Dual Energy X-Ray Absorptiometry". It measures bone mineral density, and is popularly performed by technologists with a general x-ray license and a small amount of additional hands-on training.

Mammography uses x-ray to visualize breast tissue. Specialized advanced training is needed to properly image the breast as it is extremely sensitive to radiation. A lot of mammography is used for cancer screening, but it can also include specialty views for additional diagnostic purposes as well as biopsies.

Ultrasound uses sound waves to visualize anatomy. Similar to radar, a transducer will emit sound waves and depending on the properties of the tissue that sound reflects off of, it can be interpreted into a digital signal to be displayed on screen. The most common ultrasound images people think of are fetal, but there are many sub-specialties that can be learned including emerging specialization in cardiac and vascular ultrasound.

Computed Tomography (CT) uses x-rays to visualize anatomy in cross-sectional views. If you imaging a loaf of bread, and then you take a slice out to inspect it from the top, you are viewing a cross-section of the bread. Imaging patients in this fashion produces additional insight to anatomical structures and disease processes, as well as higher visibility of certain tissues compared to regular x-rays. The images can also be rendered to produce reconstructions in 3-D. There seem to be never-ending advancements in this modality, and since the radiation dose is significantly higher than most diagnostic imaging, a good education is highly recommended.

MRI also images the body in cross-sectional views and in 3-D, but instead of x-rays, uses a magnetic field and radio waves. The result is better imaging for soft tissue structures like muscle, tendons, ligaments, and nervous tissue. Some shortcomings of visualization of other modalities can be accommodated for by MRI, but other modalities may be desired depending on what kind of tissue may be analyzed. Studies take a bit longer to perform, and there are additional patient safety issues like screening for metal that might be in the patient's body. The last thing you want to do is place a magnetic material inside a powerful MRI magnet.

Nuclear Medicine uses a radioactive isotope and gamma rays. The idea is for the isotope to gather at a certain tissue of interest, and it emits gamma rays that are detected by a special detector that lies near the patient. It is more of study to determine a particular tissue's function rather than a diagnostic exam of structure, and extra care must be taken when handling radioactive materials.

Radiation Therapy (or Radiation Oncology) this specialization uses x-rays at a much higher frequency than the traditional diagnostic x-ray that you are currently studying. You will learn in your radiography program how radiation can potentially harm cells, and it is something we try to avoid in general radiography, but with radiation therapy, the goal is to cause damage to cancerous cells with tightly focused multi-planar beams.

Cardiac Catheterization Lab (Cath Lab) You will be working with cardiologists in this specialty. Fluoroscopy and contrast media are used in conjunction with catheters and guidewires to specifically select and perform angiograms of the arteries supplying the heart muscle. When these vessels become occluded, a patient experiences a myocardial infarction (heart attack). The cath lab team can diagnose which vessel is occluded and most of the time, can open it back up while being minimally invasive – what once could only be accomplished by open-heart surgery.

Interventional Radiology: Similar to a cardiac cath lab technologist, the interventional technologist performs a variety of sterile procedures while assisting a radiologist. The cath lab deals with procedures involving the heart, while the interventional team deals with anything else in the body. Common procedures may include arthrograms, myelograms, angiograms, biopsies and percutaneous tube or drain insertions. The skill set is similar and the demand for technologists is high for both cath lab and interventional radiology.

PET (positron emission tomography) a PET scan is used to diagnose and treat many diseases, the majority being cancer. It is a functional study that can provide very specific information about the body's physiological changes. It is one of the less common modalities, but the combination of PET and CT provide unmatched information about disease processes which help physicians to more accurately treat the problem.

There's no right or wrong choice for which rotation you should choose. I would encourage you to choose something that interests you first and foremost. If you don't like it, you will probably not find much fulfillment in your career, not to mention, you may have a difficult time learning what you need to if you are dreading what you're studying. I would also recommend having more than one choice. Research things about each modality that you are considering such as job market, salary, and career paths to follow any particular modality. You want to consider choices that provide career longevity, financial security, and general enjoyment of whatever you decide to go with.

Chapter 16: Finalizing your Educational Experience

Whatever happens, do not get lazy during the last semester or two of your program. There is good reason for me to mention this multiple times. It happens often, and it can make or break your career. Try to avoid "senior-itis". This term is kind of funny because the first time I heard it was in high school during my senior year and I was tired of being in school. Later during my prerequisite courses for the radiography program, I learned that the suffix "itis" means "inflammation of." While simply being a senior cannot literally cause inflammation, a complacent attitude can become quite inflammatory for your career goals.

Your final semester will be filled with plenty of review and prep for the registry examination. At this point it's time, to use a running analogy, to "kick it in". During the final stretch of any race, runners do this by using the last bit of physical energy they can muster up to sprint toward the finish. If you slow down at this point, it could mean losing the race.

Just because you might appear to be as competent as a staff Tech in a radiology department doesn't mean you can afford to become too relaxed about your daily duties. There is always room for improvement. How do you perform in a trauma room? How do you perform in surgery? How do you perform on portable exams without any assistance? You should be trying to learn how to use the c-arm like you invented the thing. Break out the user-manual and learn all of the features – even the ones that most staff techs do not either use or even know about. Become an expert in your skill set.

New grads commonly admit during interviews that they are intimidated by being in the O.R. and want reassurance that they will be trained there. There will always be a learning curve for picking up how to function well in a surgical environment, but get used to physicians' expectations of you as a technologist and learn to act without having to be told what to do.

The same goes for fluoroscopic procedures with the radiologists. Since you will not be allowed to work long with an experienced tech overseeing your work for very long (if at all in some places) once hired, you should be taking advantage of the instruction you are currently receiving and getting the most experience that you can.

Try to make progress to become increasingly independent. Along with that, make sure to be accountable for your actions. Ask to perform procedures under indirect supervision and if you need assistance, just ask for it.   Take responsibility for your actions and your mistakes. When you make a mistake, as every technologist does no matter how much experience they have under their belt, own up to it and make efforts to correct the mistake.   This practice is far more respectable according to management than when technologists try to hide their mistakes or avoid responsibility. You are human and you will make mistakes.   Admitting your mistakes will ensure that you are noticed as being trustworthy and effectively seeking to improve upon your weaknesses.   This shows a potential employer they can trust you, and develops possibility for future growth in an organization.

If you haven't done so yet, make sure to thank the technologists and management at your clinical sites for allowing you to be there. Remember, hospitals are not always required to allow students to train at their sites. They have invested their paid staff's time, therefore the hospital's money, into training you to be able to perform a job that they might eventually ask you to be paid to do if you make a good impression and a position is available. Sure, you might be doing all the "grunt work" as I've heard it put by some students. But what about all the time they spent molding that insecure, overwhelmed individual that walked through those hospital doors on the very first day of your clinical rotation? Make sure to thank your instructors as well, and keep in touch with them after you graduate from your program.   Instructors often know of local job opportunities prior to public release due to their affiliation with clinical sites and could be a valuable reference for you during your job hunt.

Part III: After School

Chapter 17: Preparing for Employment

During the final weeks of your radiography program is when you should proactively market your skills. You need to be working on a resume if you do not already have one, and it would benefit you to begin building a professional network. Consider joining state associations relating to radiography. On the national level, being an ASRT member provides certain membership benefits that can be extremely valuable when looking for a position, obtaining your required continuing education opportunities, and it looks great on a resume too. You can even obtain a student membership with some benefits. To sign up, visit www.asrt.org. Employers like to see that you are involved in your field and care enough about it to do more than the bare minimum of arriving at work, punching the clock, and going home after doing just enough to get by.

If you don't already have a LinkedIn account, it is a good idea to create one. Visit www.linkedin.com to compose an online professional profile. Having your credentials and resume in digital format is a necessity and being searchable on a database in becoming increasingly more important these days. If you are thinking about applying for positions that are hours away, or even in a different state, consider recording a video interview to post to your public profile on LinkedIn. This would also be viewable by a potential employer and should highlight your skills, experience, and goals for employment. If you don't own a suit or professional attire, you should definitely purchase some prior to making your video. You will need it anyway when interviewing for positions.

While you are in your last eight to ten weeks of school, you should begin applying to local area hospitals, and consider applying to hospitals in regions that you may be willing to move to. In a perfect world, everyone would be able to be brought on full-time at the hospital that they received their student training at. The reality is that it's not always possible, and the hospital may need to select only one or two of the students there for a paid position. While I believe it would be foolish not to apply to the site of your clinical rotation under most circumstances, no one will hold it against you for applying to multiple locations in order to improve your chances for your "ideal" technologist position.

Your potential employers know that you will be applying for multiple positions, and because they understand that you have a responsibility to provide for yourself, they understand that it's not a personal dig at what you think about them... it's simply good business. Even if you don't plan on applying to a large multitude of positions, you should at least consider more than one. It would be even more foolish to put all of your eggs in one basket. You may hear promises when you're a student like "there will be a position here for you when you graduate" or "don't worry about looking for a job because we like you the best." You should avoid buying into these ideas, no matter how sincere the person telling you these things really is. The person telling you this may have the best of intentions, and it's always nice to have a little bit of encouragement, but they cannot predict the future. I have seen hospital staffing budgets change overnight. A well-intended promise from today could end up disastrous for you tomorrow. Do you think the person making these promises has enough influence over the hospital's finances to back up their promises? Don't be one of the only graduates without a job because you failed to apply to more than one location.

If you accept my advice and are fortunate enough, you may have more than one job offer and you will need to make a decision looking at all of the options that each job offer can provide. You may be asked about other job offers during an interview, and you may even be able to use this information as leverage for negotiating salary, a practice that is far under-utilized amongst new grads, but that's a topic for another book. The only thing you can lose by not applying to multiple positions is the amount of time it took you to apply and/or interview. You are going to have a few weeks to spare between the time you take your ARRT registry examination and when you are mailed your official results. Why not make the best of that time? Compared to the rewards you will eventually reap, I don't think that's too much of a sacrifice while you are waiting.

Sometimes depending on the job market, you may not be offered a position right away. Depending on where you are in the country and the current state of the economy in that location, this might be a real possibility for you. I am not promising you that if you follow any number of magical steps to success that you will be guaranteed a position. What you should strive to do, however, is to make a good enough impression that you are remembered the next time a position comes available and be diligent in your efforts. I can't tell you how many technologists I have interviewed who made such a good impression that received a job offer from me a couple of months down the road after initially being passed over for the original position they applied for.

You also have to realize that even if a position is available and your interview panel decides to hire you after you are on your way home from the interview, the paperwork alone can take several weeks to process and you may not receive an answer for quite some time. Try not to get discouraged, and never be afraid to send a follow-up email to inquire if you have not heard anything.

Finally, if you are not accepted for a position initially, it doesn't mean that the potential employer is no longer paying attention to you or that they somehow thought the worst of you. You MUST maintain professionalism, gratitude, and respect when being informed that you did not get selected for the position. Some people can interview well, and know all the right answers that employers want to hear. This comes with practice interviewing for positions, but you should always thank the employer for their time and consideration even after rejection. I like to send a hand written thank you card within two days of my interview expressing gratitude for the time and opportunity to interview.

Technologists whom I have been originally impressed by and may have kept in mind for my next position can often ruin their chances by reacting emotionally when learning they are rejected for a position. And the resume that I was considering holding onto subsequently goes right into my "special filing cabinet" – the trash can. Be professional and courteous at all times and opportunities will eventually come your way.

Chapter 18: Preparing for the Registry Exam

If you're anything like I was at the end of my radiography program, you will be exhausted, overwhelmed with information, and you just want to be done with it all. By this point, you will have successfully completed your capstone course, your final exams, and you have applied to take the ARRT registry examination. You should have become familiar with the ARRT's website as well (www.arrt.org). You will manage to schedule your exam at a time convenient for you, and now the education you received in radiography school will be put to the test. This is where your pre-program search for the right school is really going to pay off.

I just want to share a little bit about the exam. It is now computer-based, which is excellent. You have three hours to complete 200 questions including every topic you studied in your x-ray program, as well as 20 pilot questions designed to evaluate new test material that does not get calculated as part of your official score. There will be math, radiographs to critique, ethical questions and much more. You may use a simple four-function calculator and scratch paper provided to you by the testing center, and there is absolutely no talking. If you are the type of person who panics, this is probably the mother of all panic moments for you. It's also the time that you should remember that you properly researched a good radiography program with excellent pass-rate statistics. Everyone feels a little nervous at this point. After all, you have just finished investing two to three years of your life toward this goal, and you simply want to do your best. To view the official radiography exam content specifications that your schools curriculum is devised from, visit https://www.arrt.org/pdfs/Disciplines/Content-Specification/RAD-Content-Specification.pdf

You will more than likely be subject to more than your share of opinions, advice, and test-taking strategies that people have to offer you than you can poke a stick at, and probably far more than you want to hear. The truth is everyone is different in regards to their methods for learning, remembering information, and being able to apply critical thinking skills in a practical way to display that you have mastered a concept. By now, you will have developed some studying and test-taking strategies that you have been successful with enough to allow you to complete your x-ray program. Don't be so quick to underestimate that achievement, and stick with what works. Now is not the best time to try something new, and this certainly is not a book about test-taking methods and gimmicks for cramming at the last minute.

I would suggest, however, that you limit the amount of time between the completion of your radiography program and the time you schedule your ARRT registry exam. This is only my opinion, but I would not encourage you to wait any longer than two months, or 60 days. One reason to schedule your exam sooner rather than later is because you are not practicing radiography on a daily basis anymore, or at least until you are actively employed. If you are not seeing what you have learned at work every day, most people tend to forget things. For example, I took trigonometry in high school in 1993, and have not used it since. I couldn't tell you the first thing about trigonometry today. This is an extreme example with a very large amount of time comparatively speaking, but to be honest, I would say that by high school graduation I had forgotten just about all of it. However, due to x-ray school and being a radiographer, I am in the habit of using algebra every day and feel very comfortable with its applications in my field.

The ideal amount of time to wait would be between two and four weeks. If possible, try to plan as little as possible between the time you finish school and take your exam. I wouldn't pass up any opportunities to interview for a job, but you will also have time as I state earlier between the exam and when you receive your official results in the mail. The main reason for waiting this long before taking your exam, as opposed to taking the exam the day after you graduate, is that your mind and body need rest. You've probably been operating on very little sleep, inconsistent hours, and fast food for two years, which is not the best scenario even for Einstein to expect to perform well on a test.

There are a number of review books that have been published which are designed to prepare you to take the registry exam, and you should plan to purchase one of them. There are two that stand out above the rest for me: *Mosby's Comprehensive Review of Radiography: The Complete Study Guide and Career Planner*, 6th Edition, published in 2012 by William J. Callaway and *Radiography PREP (Program Review and Examination Preparation)*, 6th Edition, published 2011 by D.A. Saia.

These are similar to the older edition that I studied back in x-ray school, but today they are a lot more inclusive. I do not receive any form of compensation for referring either of these books, but in my opinion, choosing at least one of these to prepare you for the registry exam is a must.

It is quite possible that your respective x-ray program will require one of these for their capstone course, so you may want to ask your program director which book the school uses before deciding to purchase one. You also want to consider how early you make your purchase. If you obtain one of these too early while you are in school, a new edition might be published by the time you reach your final semester and you will need to purchase the book for school. They will want you to have the most recent edition in most cases.

You might be asking yourself, "Why do I need a review book with a bunch of sample questions if I already learned everything I need to know from the textbooks in school?" Great question! It might help to learn how the exam questions are created for your answer.

I was fortunate enough to be a volunteer to be an "item writer" (or test question writer) for the ARRT registry for a short time. They rely on volunteers in the field who are registered technologists to create a continuous stream of questions for submission and consideration for the exam. Each question is reviewed by a committee to determine if the question itself meets the quality and objectives that the ARRT stands by. If these questions are deemed appropriate for the exam by the committee, they populate a very large question bank, and there is a possibility of that question ending up in front of a graduate taking the registry exam. There are far more questions in the bank than what you will receive on your exam, and each exam is unique being composed of randomly selected questions from the master test bank. The ARRT does this so that no two tests are exactly alike. Each test has a specific number of questions from each category outlined in the content specs, but they will never be the very same questions that your neighbor will receive.

Here's where it starts to be applicable to what kind of review book you should consider. There are literally dozens of individuals from all across the country submitting exam questions. Some are working technologists, some are educators, and some could be hospital administrators, but when you think about how many different textbooks have been written over the years, and how many combinations of those textbooks are used across the country in different programs, there is naturally some variation in the methods in which the principles are taught and the verbiage used across the country. Because of this variation, you will see questions on the registry exam that approach the same principles you are familiar with in various ways, and from different angles.

Regardless of how well you might have done on your final exam in the capstone course, you will encounter similar questions asked by different authors. As long as you have mastered the concepts and can apply them, the only other possible preparation you can participate in will get you in the habit of viewing these questions from different authors than your program instructors.

Make sure to get plenty of sleep before the test, and eat a good breakfast the morning of. Definitely, under no circumstances, should you study at all the night before your exam. You may have difficulty getting yourself to stop studying and let's face it, if you don't know it by now, it's probably not going to sink in a few hours before the exam. Try to go into it well-rested and confident. The school you attended has deemed you competent to perform the required radiographic examinations and to have acquired the educational knowledge for program completion. They have placed their own school's name, or "seal of approval" to declare that you possess the academic knowledge and skill set to be sitting in that exam chair. The hard work is over. Take a deep breath and let all of that training and studying come out when the questions call for it. You are prepared.

Chapter 19: A Job vs. Your Career

After you pass the exam and successfully land employment, you'll be excited that you are finally going to get paid for all of the things that you learned to do and that you have also been performing without getting paid. I worked about 70 hours a week on average during school including my outside job and clinical externship. By the time I was working as a registered technologist, the mere 40 hours per week that I put in seemed like a vacation. I ultimately ended up working one full-time job and one casual job. I've been doing this for most of my career now, and that's one of the beautiful things about this career... the flexibility.

My program director told me something about this line of work during my last semester that I'll never forget. He said, "There's about a four to five year burn-out rate being an x-ray tech." To this day, I wonder if he intended to come across in the manner the class perceived this statement.

At the time, I thought "why didn't you tell me sooner!"

That statement was the one thing that I disagree with to this day, and perhaps it's just a matter of misperception, but he himself was in the field for a majority of his life and seemed very happy. What he probably meant to say was "most people stay in a general diagnostic role for four to five years" due to the vast opportunity of advancement possibilities.

It was about my fourth year as a technologist when I began training in other modalities like computed tomography, cardiac cath lab, and interventional radiology. Eventually, I ended up right back where I started in diagnostic radiology as an x-ray tech. Some people, including myself, actually really enjoy the art and skill behind taking a plain radiograph. I know many people who have 20 or 30 years of experience who have no plans to pursue an advanced modality. To me that's evidence that I have chosen a career that is fulfilling and will provide longevity, but what distinguishes the difference between a job and a career is all in one's attitude.

Regardless if you want to stay in general x-ray or pursue advancement in one form or another, you will need to build a reputation for yourself. You might be tempted to get into a particular routine and become a little relaxed in your practices. I challenge you to make a concentrated effort to improve upon the skills you have learned. Just as skills can sometimes be lost when you do not perform them on a regular basis, the same skills can be improved with dedicated effort. Try to perfect the techniques you have learned. I have yet to see a new grad perform at the level of a technologist who has been working for 3 years and has made a proactive effort to continuously make improvements. School really prepares you to enter this work environment, but the real impression on your career will take place once you graduate and begin working.

I got my first cross-training opportunity into interventional radiology by volunteering to do something outside the norm. It happened to be a slow day in radiology when one of the interventional techs came down the hall asking one of us to assist them during a procedure by performing a water-soluble enema while the patient was sedated on their table (and while they were performing portions of their own procedure in a sterile environment). It wasn't exactly a routine scenario and it was obvious how everyone else felt about volunteering when they avoided eye contact with the IR tech. I said "I'll do it... I don't want to get sent home because we're slow anyway." I quickly gathered my supplies and prepped the bag to perform a barium enema.

I arrived in the IR suite and found the patient under a sterile drape in a RAO position (lying half-way toward their stomach) and unconscious. I managed to place the enema tip into the patient's rectum and begin filling the large intestine with contrast while the radiologist watched it fill the colon on live x-ray. He was concerned that the procedure they were conducting had possibly caused a perforated bowel – a very serious injury that would need urgent attention. It worked out well for the patient because there was no evidence of perforation, and I cleaned up my supplies and went on my way.

I found myself in the office of the manager of cardiology a few weeks later being offered an opportunity to be trained on the job in both cardiac cath lab and interventional radiology with a substantial raise. I said yes.

Similarly, I began learning computed tomography (CT) at a different hospital when the full-time technologist and dear friend underwent some chronic health problems that needed immediate attention, and we learned that she would need to be off work for an undetermined amount of time. I volunteered to help in whatever way I could, and ended up learning how to perform CT scans. I ended up in education literally because one of the students at my imaging center thought I demonstrated concepts well, and recommended me to her program director when a sudden vacancy opened for a faculty member at her school.

I could tell you many stories about how former students have found themselves in similar situations and experienced a boost in their careers. If we are not purposely thinking about ways to gain new skills and improve our expertise, we rarely find opportunities like these come along.

Cross-training is becoming increasingly rare these days due to the higher volume of schools that have formalized training in advanced modalities, but there are so many things that can be done to improve your resume to give you a competitive edge when being considered for additional opportunities, whatever they may be.

Volunteering to serve on hospital committees will give you a greater perspective on the inner-workings of the hospital and will open your eyes to issues beyond the confines of your department. Getting to know staff outside radiology is important because sooner or later, you will need a contact for something that no one in your department may know to consult with. Continue networking, even after graduation.

Get involved in the department's quality control program. Learn the routines for equipment and safety checks, as well as how often each needs to be performed. Participate in these as often as possible and don't be afraid to throw in your own suggestions if you think something could be done better or more efficiently.

Learn how to file work orders for equipment that is down. Sometimes there are tricks to equipment malfunctions that the seasoned techs will know how to remedy. Try to pick up those tricks and ask them about others that may eventually happen so you know what to do if they are away from the department.

Ask what you can do to be helpful to the lead tech or supervisor. Even during slower moments in a hospital, there may be many duties that they are responsible for that they have difficulty getting around to because of multiple responsibilities piling up.

Volunteer for the tasks that nobody wants to do. For some reason, many techs seem to avoid going to the operating room or performing certain fluoroscopic procedures. You're all getting paid to perform these, and it may be tempting to complain that you are the only person performing these particular procedures, but try to avoid doing that because you may not know it, but the people who perform your evaluations are aware that you will do anything required of you while others are selective. Those people can have their attitude reflected in their evaluations, but you will never directly know about it due to confidentiality reasons.

Basically, you should be working to become the go-to person for anything and everything in your department. Hopefully, there are a few others like you and you will have an amazing team. If you are the only one putting forth your best effort like this, it's only a matter of time before you are recognized as invaluable to the department, and the more you are needed, the more trust and respect you earn for yourself. Keep this pattern up, and opportunities will come barging through your door. Which opportunities you decide to pursue is entirely up to you.

Chapter 20: Career Pathways

In Chapter 15, you saw a glimpse of what advanced modalities are offered within the imaging sciences when considering which special rotations appeal to you. Fortunately, if you are considering pursuing an advanced modality, having ARRT registration is a prerequisite for many of them. If you are considering climbing the career ladder, there are additional career paths to be considered outside of advanced modality training.

Within the hospital, as well as outpatient imaging settings, there are leadership opportunities. After a few years of experience, becoming a lead technologist will assign you greater responsibility within your department and give you greater input and control over some departmental decisions that affect your workflow and conditions on a day to day basis. You serve as a liaison between the supervisor and your staff technologists. It's a great position to hold if you are considering a supervisory or managerial role because it allows you to experience an elevated level of responsibility and accountability. Not everyone wants to be responsible for anything more than the patient at hand, which I can completely respect. It is however a necessary step if you want to advance.

Up the chain of command lies the radiology supervisor and radiology manager. The supervisor is typically in charge of operations for multiple modalities and ensures that everyone has the resources they need to perform their jobs. A manager may share some of the roles as the supervisor, but has a greater responsibility for the department budget and managing expenses and staffing. The manager is often held accountable for patient satisfaction, and may be required to compose action plans to address any deficiencies in the department.

A director of radiology oversees multiple supervisors and managers, and may even oversee several other ancillary departments. Responsibilities for a director lie with the corporate team, and higher education degrees are typically required along with several years of management experience.

You may also consider a career in sales and marketing. There are countless medical supply companies and vendors for x-ray equipment and equipment services. The salary is usually much higher than that of a technologist, but there is usually a lot of travel required. This path, which is best occupied by the socially outgoing and charismatically persuasive, has a lot of potential for earnings.

Another travelling career destination is applications specialist. When a vendor of x-ray equipment installs newly sold x-ray rooms into a hospital, the staff will need training on the features of the new equipment. The applications specialist works closely with the sales representative to ensure that the equipment delivers the performance promised upon purchase, as well as providing the skills to utilize those features to the staff that needs it.

If you particularly enjoy seeing people learn new things, and feel that you have the capability to communicate complex ideas, then you may be an ideal candidate to teach. To test the waters, you could volunteer to be a clinical Instructor In your radiology department if you have students. You now need a bachelor's degree to teach in a classroom for a JRCERT-accredited program, but it is something that I particularly enjoy. If you would like to keep your technologist job full-time, you could always teach a course as an adjunct instructor once or twice a week as well. One other alternative is to teach CE courses. We need 24 continuing education credits every two years to renew our ARRT registration and you can earn credits for teaching also. We are always in need of educators that have a passion for the field.

If you are computer-savvy and know a little bit about networking and databases, or have the interest to learn, you can become a PACS administrator. They are responsible for maintaining accurate records and fixing any errors with exams and medical record information. They also participate in maintaining the connectivity and efficiency of the PACS interface.

Once you have enough experience to consider yourself an expert at one particular area of radiography, or an advanced modality, some technologists decide to become consultants. Typically, you need a proven consistent track record of success in a particular area, and you can monetize that success by being paid to teach others how to attain that same level of success. You are basically paid for your opinion and to coach others on methods that allowed you to achieve results.

Chapter 21: Advanced Educational Opportunities

Becoming a radiologic technologist may be enough for many people to be content in their careers, but for some, additional educational opportunities are available for just about every preference imaginable.

As stated previously, multiple advanced modality educational opportunities are being created every single day. Ten years ago, everyone cross-trained into advanced modalities. Today, there are accredited schools that have formal curriculums which meet the ARRT standards for testing and registration. These schools are mostly attended in-person and may organize a clinical rotation for each student.

There are also the bachelor degree programs in radiologic technology or radiologic sciences available. Undergrads will gain valuable education in modalities other than general radiology, as well as knowledge of statistics, management principles, economics, and public health. Programs vary at each institution, but a BS degree is becoming a highly-sought qualification for anyone hoping to advance beyond the entry-level radiologic technologist type of position.

Even more recently, schools like <u>Midwestern State University</u> have opened masters degree programs in radiologic science. With three majors to choose from, graduate students will be prepared for careers in education, administration and radiologist assistant. These areas of focus open the possibilities for versatility in career choices in the future.

With a master's in education, you can enhance your teaching skills or become a radiography program director. This is also one of the newest requirements for program directors to maintain program accreditation.

A master's in administration prepares you to go into hospital management or administration. With this degree, you will meet the minimum educational qualifications for most hospitals for upper administration positions like CEO and corporate vice presidents.

Radiologist assistant programs are relatively new as well. Physician assistant programs have been around for ages, but a radiologist assistant specializes in radiology procedures. If you have been a technologist for several years and really feel like you have a proficiency for clinical procedures and want to gain more hands-on experience without spending the time or money to become a radiologist, this is the career path for you. RA's are sometimes depended upon to perform fluoroscopic or angiographic procedures, and can read x-rays as well. There are variations from state to state about the limitations of a radiologist assistant compared to a physician, but this should be the next up and coming profession in the imaging sciences.

The internet and learning platforms like Blackboard have made online learning possible for anyone with internet access. Depending on your style of learning, all of these educational path ways may be found on-campus, and many are now offered online. Usually there is at least a small amount of in-person attendance required, but the flexibility of options is continuing to grow.

There are generally two thought processes when deciding when to pursue advanced degrees. Some people like to take out school loans up front and go straight through school to complete their master's degrees. Others believe you should gain a few years of experience as a tech before moving on to the next level. I like to think that it is a matter of preference because everyone ends up at the same destination.

Conclusion:

If you ultimately decide to pursue a career in radiography, or if you have already made that decision, I would like to congratulate you and welcome you on a journey toward a career that has been very good to a lot of people including myself. We are in need of assertive technologists who possess an aptitude for patient-centered care. You will find yourself challenged by new situations on a daily basis, and you will have a chance to make a positive contribution to the care of patients in need.

I hope that you have found this book to be informative with a transparent view of the field to ensure your success. Whether you have chosen to pursue radiography school, or to move onto another occupation that better suits your preference, I want to thank you for reading this book. I hope it has been a valuable resource to you in your decision-making process. If you happen to run across anyone who is contemplating a career in radiography, please feel free to pass on my contact information.

ABOUT THE AUTHOR

Jeremy Enfinger BS, RT(R)

Jeremy has been a registered radiologic technologist since May of 2000. He has experience in general diagnostic radiography, CT, interventional radiology and cardiac cath lab, and has enjoyed teaching radiography in JRCERT-accredited programs since 2005. While he currently works full time as a lead technologist, Jeremy still teaches as an adjunct instructor one to two nights per week, and enjoys seeing students learn.

Author of the blog, "Topics in Radiography", Jeremy promotes collaborative interaction with students and technologists in the field while providing informational products to the community. He has written test items for the national ARRT registry examination, as well as continuing education courses approved by the ASRT. Currently, he participates in multiple committees and quality initiatives in both the hospital setting, as well as the educational system.

Contact Information:

TopicsInRadiography@gmail.com

LinkedIn
http://www.linkedin.com/profile/view?id=327973
82&locale=en_US&trk=tab_pro

Facebook Page:
http://www.facebook.com/topicsin.radiography.3

Twitter:

Topics In Radiography Blog:
http://bloggingradiography.blogspot.com

Address:

7040 Avenida Encinas
Suite 104
Carlsbad, CA 92011

Your Radiography Resource, Jeremy Enfinger

Made in United States
North Haven, CT
20 October 2022

25674011R10078